A Symphony of Remembrance
Stefan A. Carter

FIRST EDITION

THE AZRIELI FOUNDATION · www.azrielifoundation.org

A version of Stefan Carter's memoir was previously published as *From Warsaw to Winnipeg: A Personal Tale of Two Cities* by Mosaic Press. Permission for this new edition was granted by Mosaic Press and Stefan Carter.

Cover design by Endpaper Studio · Book design by Mark Goldstein · Interior map by Julie Witmer Custom Map Design · Endpaper maps by Martin Gilbert · Family tree by Keaton Taylor.

Translations of letters on pages 38–41 by Jerzy Giebułtowski. Photo 3 on page 136 and photo 1 on page 137 courtesy of the Righteous Among the Nations database, Yad Vashem, Jerusalem, ID 14468193 and ID 14468194. Article clippings on page 137 in the public domain; first published in *Nasz Przegląd* (Our Review), Warsaw, Poland, 1930 and 1933. Image of painting by Stanisława Centnerszwerowa on page 137 courtesy of the collections of the E. Ringelblum Jewish Historical Institute.

LIBRARY AND ARCHIVES CANADA CATALOGUING IN PUBLICATION

A symphony of remembrance / Stefan A. Carter.
    Carter, Stefan A., author. Azrieli Foundation, publisher.
The Azrieli series of Holocaust survivor memoirs; XV
Includes bibliographical references and index. Updated edition.
Canadiana (print) 20230205992 · Canadiana (ebook) 20230206034
ISBN 9781998880027 (softcover) · ISBN 9781998880034 (PDF)
ISBN 9781998880041 (EPUB)
LCSH: Carter, Stefan A. LCSH: Holocaust, Jewish (1939-1945) — Poland — Warsaw — Personal narratives. LCSH: Holocaust survivors — Canada — Biography. LCSH: Physicians — Manitoba — Biography. CSH: Polish Canadians — Biography. LCGFT: Autobiographies.

LCC DS134.72.C37 A3 2023   DDC 940.53/18092—dc23

PRINTED IN CANADA

A Symphony of Remembrance

THE AZRIELI SERIES OF HOLOCAUST SURVIVOR MEMOIRS: PUBLISHED TITLES

ENGLISH TITLES

Judy Abrams, *Tenuous Threads/* Eva Felsenburg Marx, *One of the Lucky Ones*

Amek Adler, *Six Lost Years*

Ferenc Andai, *In the Hour of Fate and Danger*

Molly Applebaum, *Buried Words: The Diary of Molly Applebaum*

Claire Baum, *The Hidden Package*

Bronia and Joseph Beker, *Joy Runs Deeper*

Tibor Benyovits, *Unsung Heroes*

Pinchas Eliyahu Blitt, *A Promise of Sweet Tea*

Max Bornstein, *If Home Is Not Here*

Sonia Caplan, *Passport to Reprieve*

Felicia Carmelly, *Across the Rivers of Memory*

Judy Cohen, *A Cry in Unison*

Tommy Dick, *Getting Out Alive*

Marie Doduck, *A Childhood Unspoken*

Marian Domanski, *Fleeing from the Hunter*

Anita Ekstein, *Always Remember Who You Are*

Margalith Esterhuizen, *A Light in the Clouds*

Leslie Fazekas, *In Dreams Together: The Diary of Leslie Fazekas*

John Freund, *Spring's End*

Susan Garfield, *Too Many Goodbyes: The Diaries of Susan Garfield*

Myrna Goldenberg (Editor), *Before All Memory Is Lost: Women's Voices from the Holocaust*

René Goldman, *A Childhood Adrift*

Elly Gotz, *Flights of Spirit*

Ibolya Grossman and Andy Réti, *Stronger Together*

Pinchas Gutter, *Memories in Focus*

Anna Molnár Hegedűs, *As the Lilacs Bloomed*

Rabbi Pinchas Hirschprung, *The Vale of Tears*

Bronia Jablon, *A Part of Me*

Helena Jockel, *We Sang in Hushed Voices*

Eddie Klein, *Inside the Walls*

Michael Kutz, *If, By Miracle*

Ferenc Laczó (Editor), *Confronting Devastation: Memoirs of Holocaust Survivors from Hungary*

Eva Lang, David Korn and Fishel Philip Goldig, *At Great Risk: Memoirs of Rescue during the Holocaust*

Nate Leipciger, *The Weight of Freedom*

Alex Levin, *Under the Yellow & Red Stars*

Rachel Lisogurski and Chana Broder, *Daring to Hope*

Fred Mann, *A Drastic Turn of Destiny*

Michael Mason, *A Name Unbroken*

Leslie Meisels with Eva Meisels, *Suddenly the Shadow Fell*

Leslie Mezei, *A Tapestry of Survival*

Muguette Myers, *Where Courage Lives*

David Newman, *Hope's Reprise*

Arthur Ney, *W Hour*

Felix Opatowski, *Gatehouse to Hell*

Marguerite Élias Quddus, *In Hiding*

Maya Rakitova, *Behind the Red Curtain*

Henia Reinhartz, *Bits and Pieces*

Betty Rich, *Little Girl Lost*

Paul-Henri Rips, *E/96: Fate Undecided*

Margrit Rosenberg Stenge, *Silent Refuge*

Steve Rotschild, *Traces of What Was*

Judith Rubinstein, *Dignity Endures*

Martha Salcudean, *In Search of Light*

Kitty Salsberg and Ellen Foster, *Never Far Apart*

Morris Schnitzer, *Escape from the Edge*

Joseph Schwarzberg, *Dangerous Measures*

Zuzana Sermer, *Survival Kit*
Rachel Shtibel, *The Violin/* Adam Shtibel, *A Child's Testimony*
Maxwell Smart, *Chaos to Canvas*
Gerta Solan, *My Heart Is At Ease*
Zsuzsanna Fischer Spiro, *In Fragile Moments/* Eva Shainblum, *The Last Time*
George Stern, *Vanished Boyhood*
Willie Sterner, *The Shadows Behind Me*
Ann Szedlecki, *Album of My Life*

William Tannenzapf, *Memories from the Abyss/* Renate Krakauer, *But I Had a Happy Childhood*
Elsa Thon, *If Only It Were Fiction*
Agnes Tomasov, *From Generation to Generation*
Joseph Tomasov, *From Loss to Liberation*
Leslie Vertes, *Alone in the Storm*
Anka Voticky, *Knocking on Every Door*
Sam Weisberg, *Carry the Torch/* Johnny Jablon, *A Lasting Legacy*

TITRES FRANÇAIS

Judy Abrams, *Retenue par un fil/* Eva Felsenburg Marx, *Une question de chance*
Molly Applebaum, *Les Mots enfouis: Le Journal de Molly Applebaum*
Claire Baum, *Le Colis caché*
Bronia et Joseph Beker, *Plus forts que le malheur*
Max Bornstein, *Citoyen de nulle part*
Tommy Dick, *Objectif: survivre*
Marian Domanski, *Traqué*
John Freund, *La Fin du printemps*
Myrna Goldenberg (Éditrice), *Un combat singulier: Femmes dans la tourmente de l'Holocauste*
René Goldman, *Une enfance à la dérive*
Pinchas Gutter, *Dans la chambre noire*
Anna Molnár Hegedűs, *Pendant la saison des lilas*
Helena Jockel, *Nous chantions en sourdine*
Michael Kutz, *Si, par miracle*
Nate Leipciger, *Le Poids de la liberté*
Alex Levin, *Étoile jaune, étoile rouge*
Fred Mann, *Un terrible revers de fortune*
Michael Mason, *Au fil d'un nom*
Leslie Meisels, *Soudain, les ténèbres*
Muguette Myers, *Les Lieux du courage*

Arthur Ney, *L'Heure W*
Felix Opatowski, *L'Antichambre de l'enfer*
Marguerite Élias Quddus, *Cachée*
Henia Reinhartz, *Fragments de ma vie*
Betty Rich, *Seule au monde*
Paul-Henri Rips, *Matricule E/96*
Margrit Rosenberg Stenge, *Le Refuge du silence*
Steve Rotschild, *Sur les traces du passé*
Kitty Salsberg et Ellen Foster, *Unies dans l'épreuve*
Zuzana Sermer, *Trousse de survie*
Rachel Shtibel, *Le Violon/* Adam Shtibel, *Témoignage d'un enfant*
George Stern, *Une jeunesse perdue*
Willie Sterner, *Les Ombres du passé*
Ann Szedlecki, *L'Album de ma vie*
William Tannenzapf, *Souvenirs de l'abîme/* Renate Krakauer, *Le Bonheur de l'innocence*
Elsa Thon, *Que renaisse demain*
Agnes Tomasov, *De génération en génération*
Leslie Vertes, *Seul dans la tourmente*
Anka Voticky, *Frapper à toutes les portes*
Sam Weisberg, *Passeur de mémoire/* Johnny Jablon, *Souvenez-vous*

The Azrieli Foundation's Holocaust Survivor Memoirs Program

Naomi Azrieli, Publisher

Jody Spiegel, Program Director
Arielle Berger, Managing Editor
Catherine Person, Manager and Editor of French Translations
Catherine Aubé, Editor of French Translations
Matt Carrington, Editor
Devora Levin, Editor and Special Projects Coordinator
Marc-Olivier Cloutier, Manager of Education Initiatives
Nadine Auclair, Coordinator of Education Initiatives
Michelle Sadowski, Educator
Elin Beaumont, Community and Education Initiatives
Elizabeth Banks, Digital Asset Curator and Archivist

Mark Goldstein, Art Director

Contents

Series Preface   xi
Editorial Note   xiii
Introduction *by Katarzyna Person*   xv
Foreword *by Joel Carter and Andrew Carter*   xxvii

Map   xxxi
Family Tree   xxxii–xxxiii
Acknowledgements   xxxvii

Author's Preface   1
Steeped in Culture   3
Integrated and Separated   13
Trapped   21
No Longer a Child   33
The Tide of War   45
In the Aftermath   51
Learning Experiences   63
New States and Studies   75
Rediscovering Winnipeg   85
Meaningful Work and Travels   97
Retracing the Past   103

Returning to Music   113
Epilogue   117

Glossary   127
Photographs   133
Appendix: Dealing With the Legacy of the Holocaust   147
Index   157

Series Preface:
In their own words...

In telling these stories, the writers have liberated themselves. For so many years we did not speak about it, even when we became free people living in a free society. Now, when at last we are writing about what happened to us in this dark period of history, knowing that our stories will be read and live on, it is possible for us to feel truly free. These unique historical documents put a face on what was lost, and allow readers to grasp the enormity of what happened to six million Jews — one story at a time.

David J. Azrieli, C.M., C.Q., M.Arch
Holocaust survivor and founder, The Azrieli Foundation

Since the end of World War II, approximately 40,000 Jewish Holocaust survivors have immigrated to Canada. Who they are, where they came from, what they experienced and how they built new lives for themselves and their families are important parts of our Canadian heritage. The Azrieli Foundation's Holocaust Survivor Memoirs Program was established in 2005 to preserve and share the memoirs written by those who survived the twentieth-century Nazi genocide of the Jews of Europe and later made their way to Canada. The memoirs encourage readers to engage thoughtfully and critically with the complexities of the Holocaust and to create meaningful connections with the lives of survivors.

Millions of individual stories are lost to us forever. By preserving the stories written by survivors and making them widely available to a broad audience, the Azrieli Foundation's Holocaust Survivor Memoirs Program seeks to sustain the memory of all those who perished at the hands of hatred, abetted by indifference and apathy. The personal accounts of those who survived against all odds are as different as the people who wrote them, but all demonstrate the courage, strength, wit and luck that it took to prevail and survive in such terrible adversity. The memoirs are also moving tributes to people — strangers and friends — who risked their lives to help others, and who, through acts of kindness and decency in the darkest of moments, frequently helped the persecuted maintain faith in humanity and courage to endure. These accounts offer inspiration to all, as does the survivors' desire to share their experiences so that new generations can learn from them.

The Holocaust Survivor Memoirs Program collects, archives and publishes select survivor memoirs and makes the print editions available free of charge to educational institutions and Holocaust-education programs across Canada. They are also available for sale online to the general public. All revenues to the Azrieli Foundation from the sales of the Azrieli Series of Holocaust Survivor Memoirs go toward the publishing and educational work of the memoirs program.

~

The Azrieli Foundation would like to express appreciation to the following people for their invaluable efforts in producing this book: Andrew Carter, Joel Carter, Stephanie Corazza, Mark Duffus (Maracle Inc.), Barbara Engelking, Belle Jarniewski, Céline Parent, Alison Strobel and the team at Second Story Press.

Editorial Note

This revised, updated edition of Stefan Carter's memoirs contains a new introduction, foreword, map, family tree, glossary, photo section and appendix with a list of sources Stefan Carter drew on for his research. The memoir contains terms, concepts and historical references that may be unfamiliar to the reader. English translations of foreign-language words and terms have been added to the text, and parentheses have been used to include the names and locations of present-day towns and cities when place names have changed. The editors of this memoir have worked to maintain the author's voice and stay true to the original narrative while maintaining historical accuracy. General information on major organizations, significant historical events and people, geographical locations, religious and cultural terms, and foreign-language words and expressions that will help give context to the events described in the text can be found in the glossary beginning on page 127.

Introduction

The author of this memoir, Holocaust survivor Stefan Carter, describes his story as "a tale of two cities."[1] The first city he refers to in this "tale" is his pre-war hometown of Warsaw. The second, postwar Winnipeg. For Carter, the two cities are separated by both space and time, but form two key elements of his life journey.

However, this duality in Stefan Carter's life appears much earlier. The first "tale of two cities" to appear in his memoir is the divided Warsaw of his childhood. Pre-war Warsaw, with its Jewish population ranging between 320,000 and 370,000, was undoubtedly the European centre of Jewish life. Jewish Warsaw was the site of extensive cultural and political activity, brimming with Jewish scholars, political activists, aspiring writers and musicians. It was the seat of all major Jewish parties, youth movements and trade unions, the location of performance spaces and research centres, and home to Jewish journalists and publishing houses. Leszno Street, where Stefan grew up, was the centre of Jewish Warsaw, a vibrant street filled with Jewish shops, cafés, restaurants and theatres. Yet, Stefan's story is not of the bustling Jewish life of the Northern Quarter. Even though the vast majority of its Jewish inhabitants remained traditional, Warsaw was

---

1 A reference to the historical novel *A Tale of Two Cities* by Charles Dickens, published in 1859.

also the most assimilated Jewish city in a newly independent Poland. This assimilated Jewish city was Stefan's Warsaw.

In his memoir Stefan poignantly notes, "When I was younger, I wasn't always aware that my family was Jewish." While his grandfather, a lawyer, works pro bono representing Jewish clients in courts and is a member of the illustrious Great Synagogue on Tłomackie Street, Stefan's environment is very different. His parents' generation was already married exclusively into strongly assimilated Jewish families. Both men and women were very well educated and had professional careers, which they carried out in mainly non-Jewish circles. Among his extended family are famous painter Stanisława Centnerszwerowa, his aunt; composer and music pedagogue Maksymilian Centnerszwer, his paternal uncle; socialist activist, politician and member of the Polish Legions Adam Pragier, his second cousin; and ophthalmologist and lieutenant colonel in the Polish Army Medical Corps Edmund Rosenhauch, his maternal uncle.

The most visible aspect of progressive acculturation was linguistic polonization.[2] Although pre-war Warsaw was the largest Yiddish-speaking community in Europe, Stefan did not speak Yiddish and recalled not understanding his paternal grandparents when they spoke it at home between themselves. As he wrote: "My immediate family spoke only Polish. We were deeply immersed in Polish culture and at least some members of the family held strong patriotic sentiments."

---

2 On assimilation and its components see: Todd Endelman, "Assimilation," in *The YIVO Encyclopedia of Jews in Eastern Europe*, vol. 1, ed. G. D. Hundert (New Haven: Yale University Press, 2008), 81; Katrin Steffen, *Jüdische Polonität. Ethnizität und Nation im Spiegel der polnischsprachigen jüdischen Presse 1918–1939* (Göttingen: Vandenhoeck & Ruprecht, 2004); Anna Landau-Czajka, *Syn będzie Lech … Asymilacja Żydów w Polsce międzywojennej* (Warszawa: Neriton, 2006). See also Chone Schmeruk, "Hebrew-Yiddish-Polish: A Trilingual Jewish Culture," in *The Jews of Poland Between Two World Wars*, ed. I. Gutman, 285–311 (London: University Press of New England, 1989).

Another outcome of the growing acculturation was a gradual secularization of the Jewish community. This was especially common in assimilated intelligentsia families, where children went to secular Jewish schools and wanted to conform to their peers. As a result, children brought up in atheist homes, or those that did not pay much notice to religion, often had much more contact with the Polish Catholic faith than with Judaism. Carter relates that his immediate family did not observe Jewish holidays, and that only one of his aunts fasted on Yom Kippur. Like many Jewish children from those circles, however, he did recall walking past numerous Catholic churches on the streets of Warsaw and hearing about Catholicism from non-Jewish nannies.

Carter enjoyed a childhood of a well-off middle-class Varsovian family, with music classes, visits with his father to the U Fukiera restaurant in the Old Town Market Square, frequenting theatres and opera, Sunday walks in the capital's most significant parks, summers with cousins in the resorts on the Baltic seaside and winters in the Tatra Mountains.

An important place that shaped his identity was the secular Jewish school system. After more than a hundred years of partition, Poles finally had their own free educational system, through which they were allowed to teach the Polish language alongside a syllabus imbued with patriotism. Concurrently, private Jewish schools were gradually submitting to the growing current of acculturation and introducing into their curriculum an increasing amount of Polish literature and culture. In many cases this patriotic education was strengthened even further by the family tradition that championed a "romantic" vision of assimilation.

Stefan's life was steeped in Polish culture. Describing his school, Carter writes, "It was a Jewish school for boys, and all our courses were taught in Polish. In religious class, we learned the history of the Jews. One could take Hebrew language as an optional course, but my mother thought that it would result in too heavy an academic load for me.... My uncle Maks taught us music and helped with our choir rehearsals, particularly of various Polish patriotic songs that we sang at assemblies for national holidays such as National Independence Day on November 11 and Constitution Day on May 3."

The key figure that appears in his childhood memories linked to Polish culture is Adam Mickiewicz. Mickiewicz, the great icon and *wieszcz* (prophet) of Polish Romanticism, was the most widely read poet in interwar Poland. For the Polish Jewish community, his work had a special significance as the poet's Jewish affinities made him a symbol of Polish-Jewish unity.

Yet, Stefan's family's assimilation is different from the integration-ist patterns seen in Western Europe, mainly because assimilating Jewish families could never fully merge with the non-Jewish Polish community. Assimilating individuals were universally rejected by an-tisemites, who saw them as threatening and a source of competition, and also by the majority of Jews who often considered assimilation to be a form of apostasy. Testifying to the limits of Jewish assimila-tion in the growing antisemitism of interwar Poland, Stefan Carter's childhood social environment consists almost exclusively of other assimilated Jewish families. Thus, most scholars of this period under-line the "in-between" status of assimilated Jews in interwar Poland — a group stuck between the Polish and Jewish community and, with a few exceptions, not fully accepted by either. And indeed, Stefan's memoirs also reflect on this rejection, as he describes his uncle, a very successful medical practitioner, strongly pressured at work to convert to Christianity to advance his career, and a cousin, a univer-sity student, only allowed to participate in lectures sitting in benches designated for Jewish students.

Interwar Jewish assimilation should therefore be seen not as a movement over the generations from one form of group identity to another, but rather as a movement into a state of ambivalence, where no one culture or identity can be considered to be one's own and where one's position in society remains ambiguous.

However, with the outbreak of World War II on September 1, 1939, the family's identity was chosen for them. Stefan's family, and other assimilated Jewish families, was classified as Jewish and subjected to anti-Jewish policies.[3]

After the Germans entered Warsaw on September 29, 1939, the family was immediately faced with initial acts aimed at humiliating the Jewish population. The most infamous one, the edict ordering all Jews to wear an armband with a Star of David, was only the first of an escalating number of anti-Jewish laws, which gradually separated Jews from Polish communal and cultural life. Restrictions included not walking on the most affluent Polish streets, not sitting on the public benches, not entering the public parks and not taking books from libraries or buying books in bookshops. Another group of restrictions were those aimed at the professional segregation of "Aryan" and "non-Aryan" parts of society. The Jewish intelligentsia functioning in a mixed Polish-Jewish environment, such as Stefan's family, their friends and relatives, became the first victims of the Nazi objective of pauperizing the Jews.

Yet, it took a while for Stefan to really begin feeling the persecution. He was clearly sheltered by his parents, who attempted to give him, for as long as possible, the facade of a normal youth. While Jewish schools remained closed, he continued his education by attending private classes with his former school friends.

In Stefan's memoirs, this semblance of normality is unfolding alongside his parents' desperate attempts at survival: trying to figure out if they should stay in German-occupied Poland or escape to the territory occupied by the Soviet Union, attempting to find out the fate of missing cousins, their uncertainty about the nature of the looming

---

3 On this see Katarzyna Person, *Assimilated Jews in the Warsaw Ghetto, 1940–1943* (Syracuse: Syracuse University Press, 2014).

rumours regarding setting up of the Warsaw ghetto, lack of clarity regarding German policies and their ultimate aim.

The second "tale of two cities" begins with the closure of the ghetto and the physical division between Jewish and non-Jewish Warsaw.[4] In August 1940, Ludwig Leist, the newly nominated municipal district governor, ordered all Jews to move out of the German part of the city, while all Jews moving to Warsaw were only allowed to settle in the newly defined Jewish Quarter, not in the Polish and German ones. Even though Jews were still allowed to stay in their apartments on the "Aryan" side, this was widely regarded in occupied Warsaw as a step toward the enclosure of the ghetto.

On October 2, Warsaw district governor Ludwig Fischer signed an official document ordering the creation of the ghetto; the order was made public ten days later and 113,000 Poles and 138,000 Jews were given until the end of the month to move into their respective quarters. People reacted with panic, and even the most assimilated Jews, including many of those who never wore armbands, decided to move into the ghetto. Fear of repercussions is cited in many diaries as the principal motivating factor, but there was certainly also an element of safety offered by enclosure within the ghetto walls. Although people felt a nostalgia for pre-war Warsaw, the city under Nazi occupation was viewed with fear and loathing. Most diarists saw the "Aryan" side as an increasingly threatening place and, at least until mid-1942, felt safer staying in the ghetto. Yet it seems that the realization of the

---

4 On the Nazi ghettoization policy in occupied Poland see Dan Michman, *The Emergence of Jewish Ghettos during the Holocaust*, trans. L. J. Schramm (Cambridge: Cambridge University Press, 2011) and "The Polish Ghettos," in Christopher R. Browning, *The Origins of the Final Solution: The Evolution of Nazi Jewish Policy, September 1939–March 1942*, 111–68 (London: William Heinemann, 2004). The authoritative work on the Warsaw ghetto is Barbara Engelking and Jacek Leociak, *The Warsaw Ghetto: A Guide to the Perished City*, trans. E. Harris (New Haven: Yale University Press, 2009).

weight of this decision was often recognized only after the enclosure of the ghetto, as the sheer speed of events between the announcement of the ghettoization decree on October 12 and the end of resettlement on November 15 did not give them much time for reflection.

Stefan's family, whose apartment was outside the area of the newly established ghetto, had to find a new place to live within its borders. The family finally found a room in a shared apartment on Elektoralna Street, in a section of the ghetto where people who were better off lived. Stefan recalled, "We were not starving, although there were some hardships. There were shortages of coal for heating in the winter, so we piled many layers of clothing and blankets on our beds and would even put a weighty object such as a small chair on top to try and keep warm."

As the Germans authorities continuously altered the borders of the ghetto, reducing the available living space, this added further to the family's difficulties. In the autumn of 1941, the building in which the family lived was excluded from the ghetto. The family moved again, this time to a small apartment on Chłodna Street. While Carter writes about extreme poverty surrounding them, he admits that they were particularly lucky. "While these horrific events were taking place, some people, like my family, were better off, and life continued to go on for us in some ways," he writes.

There is no doubt that assimilated Jews' pre-war professional standing, financial situation and especially contacts on the "Aryan" side created the impression that they were in a much more fortunate position than other inhabitants of the Warsaw ghetto. Testimony and memoirs from the Warsaw ghetto demonstrate that this was not the case, as the preponderance of assimilated and acculturated ghetto inhabitants fully shared the same general fate. However, among this group were those whose living standards were indeed, even if only at the beginning, starkly different from the poverty of the ghetto street. In the best situation were those who were well off before the war and were not cut off from their pre-war assets. These were adequate to sustain them through two years of living in the ghetto. Some of them managed to smuggle a large part of their pre-war assets into the ghetto; others lived off what they left for safekeeping with trusted people on the other side of the wall. In the ghetto, most of these individuals remained within their small circle of acquaintances of similar backgrounds and had very little contact with other ghetto inhabitants. They were part of the minority who, even in those circumstances, could still keep up the pretense of the pre-war way of living.

Stefan Carter writes about being surrounded by youth from the same background, teenagers who kept participating in education, usually run by the pre-war teachers from their schools, who attended language classes and met up socially. He also spent some time participating in the activities of Toporol (the Society for Supporting Agriculture), an organization for youth that maintained small plots of land within the ghetto to grow vegetables in an effort to add to the meagre foodstuffs that were available, and to introduce some greenery into the ghetto environment, which lacked parks.

Like many other assimilated families, Carter's family had contacts with the German-imposed Jewish administration of the ghetto, the Jewish Council (Judenrat). The Judenrat was to become, as a result of its overblown bureaucratic structure, the most prominent job provider for the educated assimilated strata of the ghetto. The widespread opinion in the ghetto, confirmed by those employed there, was that the main prerequisites for getting jobs in the Council were pre-war contacts. Stefan's father was working in the supply department of the Jewish Council, assisting in making artificial honey from sugar. As Stefan writes, "Sometimes he brought home some of the honey for us. We were among those with some means, more so than the majority of the ghetto residents."

Members of the assimilated intelligentsia, officers from the Polish army and lawyers were also over-represented among recruits to the ghetto police — the Jewish Order Service. The highest ranks of the Service were filled exclusively by converts and highly assimilated

Jews, and it was often claimed that with the creation of the police the divide between the assimilated and non-assimilated truly became an institutionalized part of the everyday life of the ghetto. Against the background of the traditional, religious ghetto street, the Jewish policeman represented the quintessential outsider. Stefan does not wade into the controversy of the Jewish police, but he does mention a friend of his among them.

When looking at the history of assimilated Jews in the Warsaw ghetto, it is important to bear in mind that despite their progressive pauperization, they still retained access to positions in the Judenrat or the Order Service, unlike the rest of the community. In many cases, they had just enough savings to buy an essential position in a workshop, which would turn out to be a temporary protection from deportation, and they often kept some contacts on the "Aryan" side. During the final period of the existence of the ghetto, these became factors that could ensure survival.

The *Gross Aktion*, the deportation of the Warsaw ghetto inhabitants to Treblinka, caught even those with the best connections among the ghetto leadership unaware, and unprepared. Despite the growing persecution and increasingly threatening news reaching the quarter from other Jewish communities, very few seemed to believe that the largest ghetto in occupied Poland was also doomed. But on July 22, 1942, SS-*Sturmbannführer* Hermann Höfle, Deportation Coordinator for Section "Operation Reinhard" (annihilation of the Jews of the *Generalgouvernement*) in the Office of the SS and Police Leader in Lublin District, informed the chair of the Judenrat, Adam Czerniaków, that the "resettlement to the East" was about to begin. From then on until mid-September 1942, altogether between 265,000 and 280,000 people were deported from the ghetto, with approximately 20,000 to 35,000 killed in their homes, on the ghetto streets or at the *Umschlagplatz*, where Jews were forced to gather prior to deportation. Stefan was among approximately 70,000 Jews left in the ghetto after the deportations ended in September.

Through family connections, Stefan was able to escape from the ghetto, crossing the gate with a party of workers. From that moment, Stefan became part of the underground network of Jews hiding in occupied Warsaw.[5] Staying alive required good contacts, luck and access to funds, which would allow payment for a hiding place and, if necessary, paying off blackmailers. Stefan was fully aware that here again he was in a relatively good position due to his family connections. He recalled, "The arrangements, which my cousins made for me, took a lot of effort and money and undoubtedly saved my life. The funds, I believe, came in part from the earnings of my cousins and in part from the savings their parents had from before the war."

Thanks to these funds, he was able to change his appearance by affording a surgery on his nose to get more "non-Jewish" looking and also get counterfeit papers allowing him to live "on the surface," rather than constantly remain in hiding. Yet, even for those with the best contacts, reaching the "Aryan" side was just the beginning of their ordeal. After the decree of October 15, 1941, by Governor General Hans Frank, which imposed the death penalty on those discovered outside the ghetto and also on those helping them, Jews caught on the "Aryan" side were often driven to the ghetto and then shot on the spot. Those with better-quality forged papers were imprisoned in the Jewish section of the infamous Pawiak Prison, run by the Gestapo. There they waited for up to six weeks, often tortured, while the data from their "Aryan" papers were meticulously checked. The painfully high cost of remaining in hiding was also linked to constant fear of denunciation. Fear seems to be the one factor that united all of those in hiding, irrespective of their pre-war status, background or financial situation.

The pre-war and wartime "tale of two cities" concludes with the

---

5   On that see Gunnar Paulsson, *Secret City: The Hidden Jews of Warsaw, 1940–1945* (London: Yale University Press, 2002).

story of two uprisings: the 1943 Warsaw Ghetto Uprising, which leads to the total demolition of the former ghetto area, and the 1944 Warsaw Uprising, which leads to the destruction of the remaining parts of Warsaw.

After the war, like tens of thousands of other Jews, Stefan finally left Poland with his surviving extended family members following the outbreak of postwar antisemitic violence. In early 1946, he reached a displaced persons camp in Munich, a gathering space for Jews looking to rebuild their life abroad. Like many others, Carter gradually regained an important part of his life: taking university-level courses first at the UNRRA University in Munich and later a German university, while also enjoying swimming lessons, going to the opera and spending time with friends. For him, Germany becomes a liminal space between the old life in Poland and new life in Canada.

The world of Stefan's childhood in Poland was physically destroyed. The house where he was born no longer stands. The Great Synagogue frequented by his grandfather was blown up by the Germans to mark the end of the Warsaw Ghetto Uprising. His parents, his family members and his friends were murdered along with the rest of the vibrant and complex pre-war world of Polish Jews.

The new story that began for him began in the other end of the world, in a completely new environment. Still, Holocaust survivors like Stefan remained a living link between these two worlds, and proof that the world was not completely wiped out, that it continued through them and their children.

Katarzyna Person
Jewish Historical Institute
2023

Foreword

After incredibly traumatic experiences during the horrific years of the Holocaust, our father, orphaned after the war, moved from Eastern Europe to Winnipeg, Manitoba. It was in Winnipeg where he was able to reinvent himself, reclaim his agency and appreciate so much in life. When asked what he owed his survival to, he would respond that it was to people with good souls who did the right thing, often adding, "I had some luck when so many others didn't."

Early on he set an example for us of the importance of taking care of oneself, staying active and engaged with physical and creative endeavours. But it was remarkable for us to learn that this was the way he conducted himself as a young teenager, when he was in hiding outside the walls of the Warsaw ghetto, and essentially alone. Years ago, he found and read us a letter he wrote during that time, describing to his aunt how he was exercising every day, reading, and keeping up with his studies. All the time not being able to leave the safety of the apartment he was in.

He graduated from the University of Manitoba, Faculty of Medicine, in 1954 as a top-level student — when unofficial Jewish quotas were still in place in other medical schools in Canada. While doing a fellowship at the New York Hospital in 1957, he met our mother, Emilee, a forward-thinking New Yorker, and secular Jew as well. They raised us to be freethinkers, with a breadth of diverse experiences and a respect for all peoples.

Our parents were married for more than fifty years, and our father was loyal and compassionate throughout, taking care of our mother, Emilee, in ill health until her death in 2013. In these last ten years, our father lived at home alone, being surprised he had lived that long, trying to forever just be "in the moment." He was cute, and endearing. Until age ninety-four, he continued playing badminton, a sport he discovered a love for in 1981, playing games two to three times a week. In 2017, he competed in Winnipeg's Masters Badminton Championships, the oldest player to do so, and the following year, in 2018, the Manitoba Badminton Association honoured him with a Sport for Life Award. He chuckled that it was not so much for his badminton proficiency, but for his lucky longevity and dedication to the sport he loved.

On February 8, 2023, our father, Stefan Carter, died peacefully in his ninety-fifth year at his River Heights home in Winnipeg, the home he bought with our mother in 1960, and where we grew up. He was vehement that we not use the word "passing" or "transitioning" in his obituary, stating in his own words that, "I am not and never was a quarterback." As he wanted it to be said, "He went to that Great Badminton Court in the Sky" for celestial matches pending.

And it was during these last few months that he began to find a vocabulary to be able to feel and express his emotions — something that was shut down when his mother was taken from him at the *Umschlagplatz* in the Warsaw ghetto and sent to Treblinka, a Nazi death camp. Decades ago, when one of us asked him what he felt when that happened, he paused for a moment and then said, "I guess I went numb."

Using his first-hand account as well as his vast historical knowledge and research, he had lectured and presented to many groups on the horrors of the Holocaust. His experiences in the Warsaw ghetto and the Holocaust are part of the exhibition *Examining the Holocaust* at the Canadian Museum for Human Rights in Winnipeg. He championed their mission, was a frequent visitor and lecturer, and worked alongside many Winnipeg-based organizations and projects that honour the memory of Jewish families that lost loved ones during the Holocaust.

Our father had been wonderfully content, active and independent in his last years. He was continually writing (though never finished) a new book he referred to as his "opus" and that he entitled *Anatomy of the Holocaust and Its Aftermaths: A Window into Human Nature*. He would often say given the ongoing terrible and horrific happenings in the world that he sadly did not hold out much hope for a species that continues to be so barbaric to its own kind.

Yet he was looking forward to this new edition of his memoir with the Azrieli Foundation — proud that his story would continue being a testament to the atrocities of the war and continue to foster Holocaust education.

Joel Carter and Andrew Carter
2023

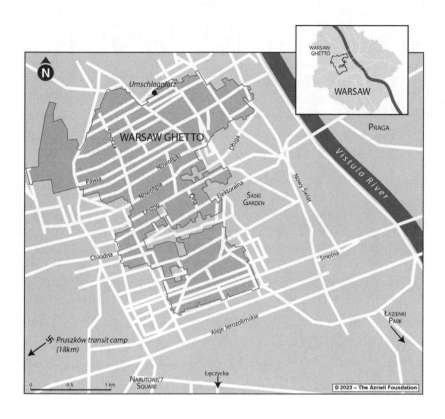

Stefan Carter Family Tree

PATERNAL GRANDPARENTS:
Juliusz* and Dora* Reicher

AUNT:
Stanisława (Stasia)* m. Maksymilian (Maks)* Centnerszwer —— *Elżbieta**

UNCLE:
Władysław*

AUNT:
Maryla

FATHER:
Wacław* m. ———————————————————————————————

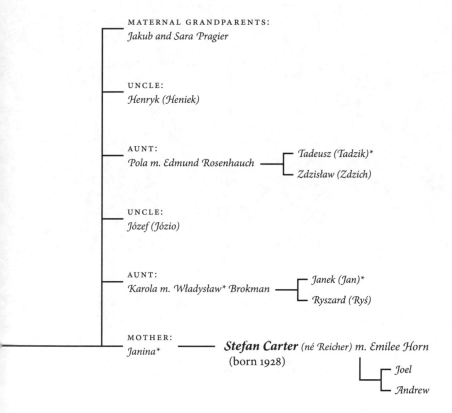

MATERNAL GRANDPARENTS:
Jakub and Sara Pragier

UNCLE:
Henryk (Heniek)

AUNT:
Pola m. Edmund Rosenhauch ── *Tadeusz (Tadzik)**
Zdzisław (Zdzich)

UNCLE:
Józef (Józio)

AUNT:
Karola m. Władysław* Brokman ── *Janek (Jan)**
Ryszard (Ryś)

MOTHER:
Janina* ──── **Stefan Carter** *(né Reicher) m. Emilee Horn*
(born 1928)
Joel
Andrew

*Murdered in the Holocaust

I dedicate this book to the memory of the members of my family who perished in the Holocaust. The world is poorer because they and millions of the Jewish population were denied the chance to make their full contribution to society.

Acknowledgements

I am grateful to the Kitzes family, who sponsored me to immigrate to Canada and opened their home to me more than half a century ago; to the University of Manitoba, where I was first a student and then a staff member, a forty-five-year relationship; to the St. Boniface General Hospital, where I was stationed for many decades, and to the technologists and other staff of the vascular laboratory there, with whom I often spent more of my waking hours with than I did with my own family; and to the granting agencies that supported my research, especially the Manitoba Heart and Stroke Foundation, whose grants I held for about three decades.

I wish to thank my wife, Emilee, and sons, Joel and Andrew, for their love and support, and for all that they taught me over the years. I greatly appreciate the support and love of my cousin Dr. George Carter of New York. I would not have survived the war if it were not for him and his parents and brother — remarkable people who play a prominent role in this story.

I appreciated the suggestions of Dr. Robert B. Tate, who read parts of an earlier draft of this manuscript. I am immensely grateful to Dr. Daniel Stone, who read the first version of this manuscript, suggested many changes and gave me the benefits of his vast knowledge and deep understanding of history.

Author's Preface

As a young boy in Poland before World War II, I was fascinated by geography and studied maps and globes with interest, and I would draw my own elaborate, detailed maps. I remember seeing the map of the British Dominion of Canada with its provinces, whose names — like Manitoba and Saskatchewan — sounded exotic to a Polish youth. I learned that Winnipeg was the centre of the wheat trade in Canada. Little did I know that a decade later Winnipeg would come to mean home, a place where I would spend the majority of my life.

This book is my personal tale of two cities. It is also the story of two countries, set in the historic context of World War II, and of two epochs spanning over seventy-five years. After the war, I was to travel over seven thousand kilometres west, from Warsaw to Winnipeg, and I would find it surprising that Winnipeg, with its much colder climate, lies almost three degrees south of Warsaw. I would discover that these two cities differed, not only in geography, but also in their social dynamics. Between pre-war Poland and postwar Canada, there was a huge difference in social structures, rights and in the appreciation of communities from various places around the world.

The world of my childhood in Poland was destroyed by the war, a war that exacted a huge price on so many peoples' lives and affected the world profoundly. Yet, large numbers of people still remain unaware of the magnitude of events that occurred during the Holocaust.

In the early 1990s, Peter Mansbridge, the anchor of the Canadian Broadcasting Corporation's national news program, reported that a survey showed that more than a third of Americans believed that the Holocaust might not have happened and were not familiar with the names of the death camps, including Auschwitz and Treblinka. The late Nobel laureate and Holocaust survivor Elie Wiesel referred to these statistics as frightening. Yet, decades later, not all that much has changed; our collective knowledge has in fact worsened. Surveys from as recent as 2018 in both the United States and Canada show that approximately 50 per cent of millennials cannot name a single concentration camp or ghetto.

There appears, therefore, a need to tell more stories of individuals' experiences from these times. It is even more urgent to make these stories known now, as the number of survivors is dwindling rapidly. The account I've written here includes my recollections of the rich life we led before war erupted in Poland. It also deals at considerable length with my postwar life in Canada. Like many of the people Hitler failed to destroy, I was able to establish a new and meaningful life after the war.

Steeped in Culture

I was born Stefan Andrzej (Andrew) Reicher in Warsaw, the capital of Poland, in 1928. One of my earliest recollections is being in my bed or crib and looking around a bright room. Elephants wearing colourful harnesses, small boys riding on their trunks, were painted on the upper walls in recurrent patterns.

We lived in a large apartment on the second floor of Leszno Street 22 in Warsaw. The three-storeyed building was large too, with three courtyards in the centre. My maternal grandfather, Jakub Pragier, a short balding man, owned the apartment. His wife, Sara, died of complications from diabetes before I was born.

My grandfather was a gentle man who was loved deeply by his five children. He was a lawyer who pled cases for poor Jewish clients in court, and he was a member of the Great Synagogue on Tłomackie Street, which I passed regularly when I attended school. He was very fond of me when I was a toddler. He carried a metal box with small round candies in his trouser pocket. I would touch his pocket and say "Ciu-ciu" (the word for candy in Polish is *cukierek*) to get him to give me one. He was also very fond of salt and apparently would salt his soup even before tasting it. When I was a few years old, he had a stroke, and he died some months later. Much later in my life, I wondered whether his fondness for salt had caused high blood pressure and led to the stroke.

My mother, Janina, was the youngest of her siblings. The oldest, Heniek (Henryk), died of tuberculosis before age thirty. Next in age was my aunt Pola, who married Dr. Edmund (Mundek) Rosenhauch from Krakow, where she moved and raised her family. Józio (Józef), their younger brother, died of complications from rheumatic fever when he was fifteen. I was told that he would spend evenings teaching young Jewish children from poor families. The second-youngest sibling was my aunt Karola. She married Władek (Władysław) Brokman in Warsaw. She died before I was born, and Władek eventually remarried a woman named Wanda, who was not Jewish.

My mother was devoted to her family; she loved her sister Pola deeply, and she nursed my grandfather during his illness. She was gentle and loving. I was the apple of her eye, overprotected and at least somewhat spoiled.

Both my mother's sisters had two sons, my older cousins, whom I greatly loved and admired. Aunt Pola's sons were Zdzich (Zdzisław Jerzy) and Tadzik (Tadeusz Edward). Aunt Karola's sons were Janek (Jan) and Ryś (Ryszard Magnus). Zdzich and Janek were more than twelve years older than me, and Ryś and Tadzik were about seven or eight years older than me. When they visited us, it always felt like a very special occasion and made me happy. I looked up to my cousins and enjoyed being with them tremendously.

Uncle Władek often sent Janek and Ryś to boarding schools abroad, and when they stayed with us during vacations, my mother acted as a substitute mother. When Ryś and I were together, we would play with armies of colourful lead soldiers. We would set them out on a large table, a "battlefield," and fight for hours. Ryś usually won, but I learned from him and was getting better. I remember Ryś's habit of repeating in whispers to himself what he had just said out aloud to me.

Though we visited Uncle Władek in his apartment in Warsaw, I did not know him well. I believe that he was quite well off. I knew Uncle Mundek much better. We visited him, my aunt Pola and my cousins in Krakow many times. Uncle Mundek, Dr. Edmund Rosenhauch to others, was a well-known and highly respected ophthalmologist and had been a lieutenant colonel in the Polish Army Medical Corps, one of the highest ranks achieved by a Jew. My uncle published many articles in medical journals, in Polish, German, French and English. He discovered a microorganism in the bacterial flora of the eye, which, he told me, was named after him for a time, *Bacterium rosenhauchii*. Apparently, when patients from Poland consulted leading European ophthalmologists in Vienna, they were told that they need not to have bothered because they had Dr. Rosenhauch available at home.

Uncle Mundek was a jovial man with a short beard, which he often stroked; he enjoyed life and loved to tell jokes. Aunt Pola was more serious, strict and highly educated. She expected very high standards from her family and from others. Uncle Mundek and Aunt Pola lived in a large villa, which included a section where my uncle saw patients. There was a garden in the back with plants and bushes. My aunt would give edible berries to passing children through the back fence. I played my first games of Ping-Pong against my cousins in their living room. Tadzik was left-handed, and he would say jokingly, "Think what I could do if I played with my right hand!"

~

My paternal grandfather, Juliusz Reicher, worked in a bank. He was a tall man who prided himself on walking very straight and often admonished me for slouching. He and my grandmother Dora played cards and counted tricks aloud, though I didn't understand the counting because it was in Yiddish. They had four children: my father, Wacław; his two sisters, Stasia (Stanisława) and Maryla; and his brother, Władek (Władysław).

Uncle Władek was an engineer who built bridges. He usually wore tall, shiny army boots. Aunt Maryla taught piano. She, like other women at the time, wore her hair in braids rolled in a bun that was pinned to the back of her head. I heard that when she let down her hair it reached to her ankles.

Aunt Stasia, born in 1889, was a well-known painter. She married Maks (Maksymilian) Centnerszwer, and they had a daughter, Elżbieta. They lived in Warsaw, on Hoża Street 49, and we would visit them there. Aunt Stasia worked in studios in Warsaw and Paris, travelling widely in France, Italy and Yugoslavia, and she would return from her travels with paintings of landscapes and architectural sketches.

Aunt Stasia was known for her portraits and post-Impressionist style landscapes, and she exhibited her work at the Salon des Indépendants in Paris, in a group exhibit of Polish artists in Barcelona and in various exhibits in Poland, including with some Jewish art groups. Her works were exhibited together with those of other artists in a huge exhibition organized by the Jewish Society for the Encouragement of Fine Arts. Articles about her appeared in the Polish Jewish newspaper *Nasz Przegląd* (Our Review), one of the leading newspapers of the time. In issue 23 of November 1929, an interviewer asked her about the culture for Jewish artists in Poland. My aunt stated that the general atmosphere in Poland at the time did affect Jewish artists, and that they hardly had any contact with the Polish artistic world, while that was not the case in other European capitals.

At one point, she was approached by Otto Schneid, an artist and art historian who was gathering materials for a work about Jewish artists. She responded to his inquiry in 1930 with a letter and a short autobiography as well as two sketches, which are now held in the archives of the Thomas Fisher Rare Book Library at the University of Toronto. Schneid spent the last ten years of his life in Toronto.

Uncle Maks, born in 1889, was a well-known violinist, composer, pedagogue and music critic. In 1914, he began teaching singing in Warsaw. His book *Śpiew* (Singing) was a required text for high school courses between the two wars. He taught music as well, and he was a respected writer and an active supporter of the Jewish Music Society and the International Society for Contemporary Music. Uncle Maks composed vocal and chamber music, including poems he titled "Tristan" and "Ballad" for tenor voice and chamber orchestra. I remember attending a concert of the Warsaw Philharmonic with my parents a few years before the war began at which his composition for a small orchestra was performed.

I took piano lessons with my aunt Maryla when I was a youngster, and I played a simple composition for four hands with her during a recital that she held for her students. I was very shy, and she was very kind. Unfortunately, my lessons with Aunt Maryla soon stopped and I did not see her again. I was not told at the time that she had died. I did take piano lessons with other teachers after that, but my progress was slow; it seems I wasn't motivated to practise diligently.

My parents both appreciated and played music. Before I was born, my mother studied music and taught piano. In our drawing room, which faced the street, there was a grand piano on which my mother practised, playing Chopin's waltzes and Beethoven's piano concertos, among other music.

After dark, I would hear the music from my room. My father, an amateur violinist, and a friend of my parents, *Pan* (Mr.) Józef, who played cello, would join my mother on the piano. My appreciation of music at the time was not equal to their repertoire, and I would scream, unable to sleep because of the noise. My mother always had to come quiet me down. The interruptions did not please Pan Józef. Could it be that they played the *Archduke Trio* by Beethoven, which was to become one of my favourite works?

My father loved music and I remember him playing on his violin and whistling the humoresque by Dvořák, which was one of his favourites. I also recall my father singing a song from *Wesele* (The Wedding) by dramaturge, painter and writer Stanisław Wyspiański. It was "Miałeś, chamie, złoty róg" (You had, boor, a golden horn) and was meant to be a symbol of the apathy felt by some of the Polish rural populace that contributed to Poland's inability to shake the might of the foreign powers and win its independence before World War I.

My family would listen to radio programs that had comedy revues. I remember the call of the Polish radio; it was the opening of the *Military Polonaise* by Chopin in A major. We heard and came to know many songs that became popular at the time. I remember singing the hit "I Have a Date with Her at Nine" ("Umówiłem się z nią na dziewiątą") by the Polish Jewish composer Henryk Wars. Jewish musicologists and musicians, my uncle Maks among them, played a considerable role in the formation of Polish musical culture, composing many popular songs.

~

My father was a chemical engineer and worked in a laboratory that was involved in testing related to the sugar beet industry. When I once visited him there, he performed what I considered to be a miracle. A colourless fluid in a beaker changed to bright crimson when he added a drop of a reagent, then it turned to a pretty blue before returning to its original colourless state. I know that he published a scientific article on estimating the temperature of metals from their colour during heating.

On one occasion, when I was a little older, my father took me to a winery called U Fukiera, which was situated in the main square in the Old Town district. Colourful houses built in an old architectural style surrounded the square. There he treated me to a small glass of delicious aged Polish mead (honey wine), a drink of the Polish gentry.

My father was very interested in sports, an interest he shared with me. We attended soccer matches of the club Polonia, of which he was a supporting member, and an international match where Poland played Germany. We followed the fortunes of the Jewish boxers: Shepsl Rotholc from the club Gwiazda (Star) and Rubinstein from Maccabi. Rotholc became a national champion in the flyweight division before the war.

We occasionally went to the movies, which were in black and white then. I saw *Modern Times* with Charlie Chaplin and several films with

Shirley Temple. I was particularly impressed with *One Hundred Men and a Girl* with Leopold Stokowski and Deanna Durbin, who I later learned was nicknamed "Winnipeg's Sweetheart" after the city of her birth. Later I saw movies in colour, like *Snow White and the Seven Dwarfs* and *The Adventures of Tom Sawyer*.

Warsaw was a vibrant city of one and a half million, referred to at times as the "Paris of the East." I attended concerts of the Warsaw Philharmonic and a Chopin piano competition with my parents. The city had a number of theatres and an opera house located at the plac Teatralny (Theatre Square), where the city hall building also stood. I went to the opera *Straszny dwór* (The Haunted Manor) by the famous Polish composer Stanisław Moniuszko. In the opera there was a chime clock that played a catchy tune. Some friends and my cousins and I would whistle part of that tune to communicate with each other.

On Sundays I often went with my parents to one of a series of parks abutting onto the major thoroughfare Aleje Ujazdowskie: Park Ujazdowski, the Botanical Gardens or Łazienki Park (Royal Baths Park). Close to the entrance of Łazienki Park stood a monument of Fryderyk (Frédéric) Chopin. Large chestnut trees bordered the broad lanes. The chestnuts were not edible, but we used to have fun gathering and playing with them. A summer palace of the last Polish king stood on a small island surrounded by an artificial lake with two connecting bridges. At the lake one could rent rowboats, and I enjoyed rowing there with my father. Nearby was an outdoor summer theatre, still there today, and the show grounds for international horse jumping competitions, which my father would take me to.

Warsaw boasted a large zoological garden located on the east bank of the Vistula River in the suburb of Praga, and my parents took me there several times. There, a few years before the war, a baby elephant was born. There was a contest to name it, which resulted in the choice of the name "Dwunasty" (Twelfth), as it was the twelfth elephant born in captivity.

We would spend our summer vacations at various resorts and often vacationed at the Baltic seaside. We would travel there by train, and I was always excited to get ready for the trip. In my early years, we went to the resort town of Hel at the tip of the Hel Peninsula. In Hel we often stayed with the families of fishermen. The fishermen in Hel would go out to sea at night in small *kuter* boats with one-cylinder engines. The fresh fish that they brought back, such as the flat flounders, were delicious when fried. We would use smoked fish to make sandwiches that we took with us to the beach.

We would walk to the beach in Hel through a forest of evergreens. The long, wide beach had beautifully fine and light-yellow sand. There I built sandcastles and played with stones and shells that I gathered in a small pail. Sometimes we found numerous transparent pink jellyfish washed ashore. The water was clear and shallow near the shore, and though I could not swim, I would wade a few feet into the water and sit down on the sandy bottom, completely submerged. The rays of the sun would play wavy, shimmering patterns on the soft sandy sea floor around me. It was pleasant to be submerged in the cool water in the heat of the sun. The adults talked as they tanned. They would put on lotion, and the women would protect their noses from sunburn with green plant leaves. Along the beach there were tall booths made of hard reeds where people could find shade and change into swimming suits. Vendors sold delicious Italian ices and ice cream that was greatly enjoyed by all. The white lemon ice was my favourite flavour.

At times, we would see large passenger ships and Polish navy ships on the horizon. We especially admired the beautiful, tall ship, the frigate *Dar Pomorza* (Gift of Pomerania), which served as a training craft for young sailors. We also saw Polish navy ships and were familiar with the destroyers *Wicher* (Gale) and *Burza* (Storm) each with three stacks, and later the new additions *Grom* (Thunder) and *Błyskawica* (Lightning) that had one wide stack.

A short walk along the beach would bring us to a tall wooden lookout tower called the Stork's Nest. We would climb to the top, where the view of the horizon was spectacular. In the evening we would stroll to the small harbour and walk on its piers, watching the passenger ships that often docked there. There were two smaller twin ships, *Wanda* and *Jadwiga*, named after the daughters of the former Polish prime minister Józef Piłsudski and two larger ones, *Gdańsk* and *Gdynia*.

A bright friend of mine, Stefan Kraushar, whose mother was a friend of my mother's since their school days together, wrote a patriotic letter to President Ignacy Mościcki, who arrived on one of the ships, and handed it to a sailor. No one expected that the letter would be given to the president. It was, therefore, a wonderful surprise when my young friend received a reply several weeks later and was invited to the palace where the president resided in Warsaw.

Our relatives from Krakow and my cousin Ryś would sometimes vacation with us, making it even more enjoyable. Together, we would carve ships from pieces of bark, using wooden matches for masts and gun turrets. My mother would buy small painted wooden toy ships for Ryś and me to play with. My cousins played a complex game involving states with people, pawns, ships and imaginary diplomacy. Tadzik had Japan, Ryś had Canada, their friend Maryś had Great Britain, and Zdzich, who was less interested and participated to a limited extent, had Monaco. I was thrilled to be given an opportunity to join and chose Sweden. On some evenings we all went to a nightclub called Polonia, where there were refreshments and dancing. My cousin Zdzich was a superb dancer and I would see many eyes in the crowd following him enviously as he danced.

For winter vacations we went to the mountains, such as the well-known resort town of Zakopane in the Tatra Mountain range. My uncle Edmund co-owned a sanatorium-hotel in the resort town Rabka-Zdrój in the region of the Carpathian Mountains, where we stayed with our family from Krakow. The view of the tall mountain peaks was impressive. In Zakopane, the tall double peak of the Giewont

Mountain was the local landmark, with the large cross erected on one of the peaks easily visible from the valley town. A fairly short drive from the town, and then quite a hike up to a higher elevation, there was a round, glacial lake, Morskie Oko (Eye of the Sea). Steep mountains with snow-covered peaks, even in summer, surrounded it, creating a breathtaking view.

My cousins Zdzich and Tadzik were excellent skiers. I later learned that Tadzik used to go on skiing trips from Krakow with a young student named Karol Wojtyła, the future Pope John Paul ii. I took some skiing lessons and tried my skills on easier slopes. In the evenings, people skated on an outdoor rink to music. Uncle Edmund was an excellent skater. When he ice danced with Zdzich or Tadzik, people would look on with wonder.

Integrated and Separated

My childhood was happy and carefree. I was an only child and my parents loved me deeply. When my parents would go out for the evening, I would feel insecure and would not fall asleep until I heard the sound of their key opening the front door when they returned. I do not know why, but when I was around six years old, I suddenly realized that life was not going to last forever, that it was finite and that one day even I would die. This realization felt unsettling, but it did not colour my outlook.

We were fairly well off, with our live-in maids who cooked and nannies who looked after me when my mother went to work. We ate well. I recall tasty meals that featured various soups; I loved borscht with delicious meat-filled knishes. The second course would be meat, potatoes and vegetables. My favourites were meatloaf that we called *klops* and brisket with browned groats (*zrazy z czarną kaszą*). I always liked potatoes, and of course the desserts and tea.

Leszno Street, where we lived, was a wide and bright street in the central part of Warsaw. From the front balcony off the living room, we would watch parades for national holidays and political events, and the final stages of the cycling races between Poland and Germany that ran from Berlin to Warsaw. The traffic included horse-drawn carriages for hire, *dorożki*, and some new taxi cars, though the most frequent mode of transportation was the red electric streetcar. A smaller balcony off the dining room opened onto a courtyard, where street musicians, violinists or organ grinders, some with a small monkey, would play, waiting for us to throw down coins (*groszy*) wrapped in pieces of paper. From the window of my room, I could see Orla Street, which led, over cobblestones, to Elektoralna Street, where my paternal grandparents lived.

Sometimes we visited my mother's relatives, her elderly aunts Leonka and Gutka. Leonka was short, rotund and jolly, and Gutka was taller, slimmer and quieter. They both liked to fuss over me. I also recall being invited to the spacious apartment of the Rechthand family, distant relatives of my mother. Zofia and Kazimierz Rechthand were wealthy and influential in the Jewish community; I remembered feeling very shy when I had once met them and their two daughters when we vacationed at the seaside resort of Orłowo. The older daughter, Genia (Eugenia), was very beautiful with dark hair, whereas the younger, Wanda, also pretty, was blond and had blue eyes. At their home we were served small sandwiches that were eaten with a knife and a fork, a custom I was not familiar with. I followed what everybody else did and that made my mother proud.

A block west of our building was Karmelicka Street, which originated from Leszno and ran north. It was full of crowds of observant Jews wearing the traditional black dress and hats. They spoke Yiddish, which I did not understand. On the street, vendors offered various wares among which were flat oblong *placki*, a sort of thin baked pancake. They were salty and deliciously browned.

Eastward from where we lived were stores, one at which we would buy a drink called *kwas*. It was different from the Russian *kwas* and consisted of soda water with a few drops of a fruit extract in it, a sort of soft drink. There was also a bakery where we would buy delicious brown rye bread. A few steps farther on our side of the street stood an impressive Protestant cathedral in the gothic style. Further east, one would pass the Great Synagogue on Tłomackie Street and then reach Długa Street. There stood the Spójnia (Union) School, which I would later attend.

At one time we took in a boarder, Mr. Waldemar Trenkler. He stayed in the room where my grandfather had lived until his death. Mr. Trenkler was friendly and showed me various stars and constellations in the night sky. How he made his livelihood we did not know, as he did not go out to work, but he spent considerable time going over the Warsaw telephone book. In 1938 we moved, without the boarder, to a smaller but very nice apartment on Smolna Street 36, close to the broad Nowy Świat Street and Aleje Jerozolimskie, where there were national art and military museums.

My early education took place in a private group with several children, run by Mrs. Helena Fishaut in her apartment. It was the equivalent of Grades 1 and 2. There were a couple of summers when I was sent to Mrs. Helena's summer camp in the Carpathian Mountains. There, under the supervision of a counsellor, we went hiking and played games and sports. I liked wandering in the forest in the shadow of tall evergreens on a soft carpet of brown needles. Often, we gathered a variety of mushrooms, a Polish pastime. That reminded me of collecting mushrooms with my parents and them not allowing me to eat any after they were cooked for supper. I was very upset and, I was later told, cried and screamed for hours.

After an active day, we looked forward to a delicious drink of cold, sour milk, made from unpasteurized milk, similar to yogurt. One game we played was called *serso*. Light wooden rings, made of thin branches, were thrown high and far in the air with a long wooden stick, and the opposing players tried to catch them on their sticks. We had Olympic-style games with different teams consisting of three members each. The sports included running and field events, like shot put, discus and jumps. At the camp were several of my childhood mates: Mrs. Helena's son Piotr and daughter Ela, Hanka Kon, Alinka Puszet, Piotr Held, Irka, and Stefan (Wojtek) Minsk, who used to try to fence with me using the *serso* sticks, which Mrs. Helena forbade.

I entered Grade 3 at Spójnia School, where my mother worked as a secretary. It was a Jewish school for boys, and all our courses were taught in Polish. In religious class, we learned the history of the Jews. One could take Hebrew language as an optional course, but my mother thought that it would result in too heavy an academic load for me. At recess we played soccer. We did not have a ball and used an old slipper instead!

My uncle Maks taught us music and helped with our choir rehearsals, particularly of various Polish patriotic songs that we sang at assemblies for national holidays such as National Independence Day on November 11 and Constitution Day on May 3. I came to know many beautiful and stirring soldiers' songs such as "We Are the First Brigade" ("My, Pierwsza Brygada"), a song of the Legions of General Piłsudski, who fought for Polish independence during World War I, and the national anthem, "Mazurek Dąbrowskiego," sung by the Polish Legions who fought with Napoleon. My favourite was "Oh My Rosemary" ("O mój rozmarynie"). The songs that we learned reflected the strong tradition of glory during the armed struggles over Poland. The Polish cavalry was famous, and the Polish hussars created havoc in many battles during the sixteenth and seventeenth centuries, a tradition that continued with the ongoing struggles against neighbouring Germany, Austria and Russia.

The principal of my school was Mr. Ramberg, whose son Jaś was a friend of mine. I was a good student, but I had trouble with literary composition. Yet I read various books, including some educational books that my father gave me, like *Godziny wieków: Historia świata dla ciebie* (*The Hours of the Ages: World History for You*) about the history of humanity and *Bracia z całego świata* (*Brothers from Around the World*) about diverse cultures. I enjoyed the subject of history the most and I found every period interesting, although I was particularly fascinated by the history of the Greeks. I can still recall verses that we read relating to the Battle of Thermopylae, one of several battles fought by the Greeks against the massive invading Persian armies.

I liked to read the magazines for young people called *Płomyk* (Flame) and *Płomyczek* (Little Flame). These magazines started publication around the time of World War I, and despite some interruptions, continued to appear after World War II, one until 1991, the other until 2013. I remember only one puzzle from the magazine, and curiously it was this:

$$\frac{K}{A} = ?$$

In Polish, the letter *k* is pronounced *kah*, the word "above" is *nad* and the letter *a* is pronounced *ah*, making the answer Kanada, which is how Canada is spelled in Polish!

I loved to read from the collected works of the great Polish Romantic poet Adam Mickiewicz, which we had at home. I enjoyed Mickiewicz's ballads and sonnets; among them the *Crimean Sonnets*, "The Three Budrys" and "Reduta Ordona," about the fall of a bastion of Polish soldiers during the uprising against Russia in 1830.

Mickiewicz had grown up in the eastern territory of the Polish-Lithuanian state and considered himself both a Lithuanian and a Polish patriot. While living in Paris, France, where he had immigrated, he wrote one of the greatest epics of Slavic, if not world, literature — *Pan Tadeusz*, which opens with a moving ode to Lithuania. To this day, I can recite my favourite passages from *Pan Tadeusz*. Among many excerpts of great beauty is the description of the "thundering" and "triumphal" concert played by a Jewish innkeeper, Jankiel, on a dulcimer, which gives a sense of how Poland's greatest poet saw a Jewish man as a Polish patriot.

I collected postage stamps, as did several of my peers, each of us focusing on stamps from one particular country. I decided to concentrate on Romanian stamps. My friends and I were also interested in collecting single negative film frames from films with cowboys played by Ken Maynard and Tom Mix. I especially remember the series of books we all read about Indians and the Wild West of North

America by Karl May. The author was German and had never set foot in America, but his imagination of that part of the world was truly vivid. Other books I read were comedies by P. G. Wodehouse; historical novels by the Polish Nobel Prize winner Henryk Sienkiewicz; a book about Canada by Arkady Fiedler; and poetry by the Jewish-Polish writer Julian Tuwim. My friends and I particularly enjoyed Tuwim's *Jarmark rymów* (*Market of Rhymes*), which was written in a witty style.

After school and on other occasions, we went to the large and beautiful Saski (Saxon) Garden in the centre of Warsaw to play. The gardens bordered the Piłsudski Square in which stood the Tomb of the Unknown Soldier. During national holidays, the gardens held parades in which army battalions and colourful cavalry regiments of Ułani and Szwoleżerowie took part. We played there with marbles and used penknives to play games in the dirt. We would also play a variant of hide-and-go-seek, which was almost always won by Piotr Held and his girlfriend, Irka. The Saski Garden had a summer theatre, where I attended some performances. There was also a pond with two white swans where we would skate in the winter using skates that we attached to our shoes. I recall one incident when we were attacked in the gardens by a group of youths with sticks and stones, possibly an antisemitic provocation.

~

When I was younger, I wasn't always aware that my family was Jewish. As a young child, my feelings about religion were ambivalent. That was largely because of the people who took care of me when my mother went to work. We had live-in maids and nannies, all of whom were Roman Catholic and talked to me about their religious beliefs. I remember feeling awkward and uncertain of how I should act when I walked by the numerous Catholic churches on the streets of Warsaw.

As I grew older, my realization about our faith took place slowly. My comprehension increased as I learned more about our Jewish background from my family members. I became aware of the existence and importance of Palestine in the aspirations of some of the Jewish people. In a naive way I wondered who I should root for if there were ever a war between Poland and Palestine. Although I was aware that I was Jewish, it did not affect my life in any practical way, largely because my family was assimilated and not religious. We did not observe Jewish holidays, although one of my aunts fasted on Yom Kippur. I do remember seeing little shacks covered with tree branches during the Jewish holiday of Sukkoth.

About 30 per cent of the population of Warsaw was Jewish. Most Jews were not well off. They made a living as tailors, traders or in small businesses. They followed an observant way of life and spoke Yiddish. Many Jews belonged to Orthodox religious groups, in which men wore distinctive black clothing and hats, and had beards and sidelocks. Their children wore similar dress.

I feel that I was fortunate in that my family was among a small group of Polish Jews, likely no more than 10 per cent, who were financially well off and mostly assimilated. My immediate family spoke only Polish. We were deeply immersed in Polish culture and at least some members of the family held strong patriotic sentiments.

Numerous assimilated Jews, including my relatives, played prominent roles in Polish cultural and political life. In addition to my aunts and uncles who were respected artists and musicians and doctors, my mother's cousin Adam Pragier, who had fought in the Polish Legions during World War I, became a member of the Polish parliament in the 1920s.

Antisemitism was rampant when I was growing up, and many Jewish children were beaten by antisemitic Polish youth on their way to school. As an adult, I learned that antisemitism was not limited to Poland or to that time period. It had existed for two millennia and has been referred to as "the longest hatred," since it started with Christian-Jewish conflicts soon after the beginning of the Christian era. But as a child, I was mostly unaware of the growing antisemitism around me.

As the years went by, though, I did learn about certain manifestations of antisemitism — my uncle Edmund was told that he would be made the chair of the Department of Ophthalmology at Jagiellonian University if he converted to Christianity, which he refused to do, and my cousin Tadzik, a medical student at the time, was subjected to the "ghetto bench," which meant that Jewish students were segregated, assigned to specific banks of seats in the lecture theatres. They refused to sit there and, in protest, stood during lectures together with some Polish students who supported them. Antisemitic Poles gave their Polish colleagues who supported Jewish students a hard time, sometimes beating them.

As the 1930s were drawing to a close, important international events were taking place, though I was not aware of them at the time. Germany annexed Austria and part of Czechoslovakia. Shamefully, Poland annexed small parcels of land from Czechoslovakia.

Poland signed a common defence act with Great Britain. As part of the act, in an operation called the Peking Plan, three of the four Polish destroyer ships, all except *Wicher*, sailed to England in late August to avoid destruction by the much stronger German naval forces in the Baltic Sea during the imminent outbreak of hostilities and to support the British Royal Navy. These Polish ships were to distinguish themselves in sea battles alongside the British Navy during World War II.

In August 1939, we were vacationing in the Tatra Mountains in the resort of Zakopane, and my aunt Pola from Krakow joined us there. We went for walks, and I played some table tennis outdoors with a friend from Warsaw. My mother and aunt were very close, and I remember that when we were saying goodbye before going back to Warsaw, they cried, as they always did whenever they parted. This time, they would never see each other again.

Trapped

Germany invaded Poland on September 1, 1939. On September 3, France and Great Britain declared war on Germany. That day, we went to the British embassy, where the Polish foreign minister, Józef Beck, appeared on the balcony with the British ambassador, a crowd gathered below.

In those first few days, while Warsaw was being bombed and many buildings were destroyed, newspapers printed special editions, reporting that French troops had broken through the German fortifications of the Siegfried Line — probably pure propaganda.

Polish authorities called on the population to leave the city and proceed eastward, away from the advancing German army. Apparently, men were going to be mobilized in the east to help fight back. I walked with my parents along a dusty road among crowds that were clogging the roads so that traffic couldn't get through. I was eleven then and remember being really scared for the first time in my life as German fighter planes flew low over the road with their machine guns blazing. We were told by passing Polish soldiers to lie in the ditches by the side of the road. As the gunfire from the planes came closer, my heart pounded heavily.

In the town of Falenica, which we reached after a few hours of walking, the thirsty throngs descended on the general store, but all that was left were bottles of vinegar, which some people drank. We got to about thirty kilometres from Warsaw and stayed in the small town of Otwock. There was a shortage of food and tobacco. My father, who smoked, was most uncomfortable and tried to satisfy his craving by smoking rolled-up wood shavings.

The Polish army resisted heroically but to no avail — it was no match for the might of Germany. Within a couple of weeks, German troops arrived in the village where we were staying. Everyone in the village was rounded up and forced to stand outside. My mother pushed me to stand near my father, hoping that would make it less likely that he would be taken away. I don't think the Germans took anybody that day.

Warsaw soon fell to Germany, and we left the village, carrying some vegetables from local farmers, and returned to our apartment in the city. We learned that a German bomb had killed our previous boarder, Mr. Waldemar Trenkler. I heard that when he had lived with us, he worked for the Germans, preparing lists of Jewish people and their addresses from the telephone book.

German authorities soon issued orders against the Jews. Signs marked "Jews Forbidden," in German and Polish, appeared at entrances to parks and restaurants. Germans confiscated Jewish property. By the end of November 1939, Jews had to wear a band with the Star of David on their right arm, which made them obvious targets of attack for Germans and antisemitic Poles. I was not aware until much later that the Germans had already begun carrying out acts of terror during the 1939 war campaign, brutally murdering Jews and some members of the Polish intelligentsia in a haphazard manner. Anti-Jewish persecution continued with individual acts of violence and humiliation. The Germans would shave off the beards of observant Jews, beat Jews and murder them on an ongoing basis.

At first, my family's life seemed to proceed at a fairly even keel, though the atmosphere was uneasy. I would go by streetcar to play with my friend Staś Kopel, but my mother was anxious when she let me go, as he lived in another part of the city. I continued my education at home, taking private lessons.

We wondered what had happened to our relatives when the war broke out, and we worried about them. Our relatives from Krakow contacted us in the winter of 1939–1940; they had made their way to Lwów (now Lviv), and they wanted us to join them there. We set out eastward by train to the border between the German and Soviet occupied areas. We arrived at night and waited in a barn for many hours to be taken across the border by a guide. Unfortunately, the border was guarded too closely and we had to return to Warsaw. Had we succeeded in getting through, who knows how things would have turned out for us.

In April 1940, Germans ordered the Jewish Council (Judenrat), which they had established, to pay forced labourers to build brick walls across streets to enclose a section of Warsaw where most of the population was Jewish, creating the ghetto. In October, the Germans issued an order that all Jews move, under penalty of death, into the part of the city within the brick walls by November 15, and that Poles living there move out. Approximately one hundred thousand Poles moved out and some one hundred and forty thousand Jews moved into the ghetto, where there were already slums. It was terribly over-crowded, and many Jewish families were forced to live with one or more families to a room.

We moved into the ghetto, into the apartment of my mother's friend Mrs. Kon, on Pawia Street, which overlooked the notorious Pawiak Prison. The day after we moved in, we found out that the ghetto was closed. We could not leave; we were trapped. I remember a very heavy feeling in my chest, a foreboding feeling.

～

The density in the ghetto increased whenever the Germans brought in more Jews from numerous nearby towns, as well as from other countries, Germany in particular. Eventually, four hundred thousand people lived in the ghetto, further increasing the unbelievably over-crowded quarters and leaving many homeless.

The ghetto was under the jurisdiction of the Jewish Council, which was accountable to the German occupation authorities. The chairman was Adam Czerniaków. My mother's relative Mr. Rechthand was one of the members. A Jewish ghetto police force, with sticks as their only weapon, was formed to help keep order. The members of the ghetto police came from various backgrounds. Among them were the boxing champion Rotholc and my childhood friend Piotr Held, who became a junior policeman.

The conditions in the ghetto were extremely harsh. Germans oppressed the Jews in the ghetto in many ways. They killed some and took others to camps, where they did heavy labour. But, mainly, they starved us. The food rations varied over time but at some point in 1941 they were reduced to about two hundred calories per day. Nobody could survive on that.

Many people, facing abject poverty, turned to begging, which became prevalent on the streets of the ghetto. Some people began smuggling in food and other items to prevent their families from starving. Smugglers would either bribe the German soldiers and Polish police who were guarding the gates to the ghetto or come in and out through gaps in the brick walls. It was usually Jewish youth who did the smuggling through or over the ghetto walls. Many of them paid with their lives when they were caught. While few people had savings or valuables that could be sold to buy food, others with more means carried on, doing business. The unscrupulous made quite a lot of money from smuggling; so contrary to what most ghetto residents were experiencing, they wallowed in luxuries and frequented elite cafés and restaurants in the ghetto.

After a brief stay in the apartment of Mrs. Kon, we moved into a room in a dentist's apartment on Elektoralna Street; people who lived in that section of the ghetto were slightly better off than people who lived in other parts. We were not starving, although there were some hardships. There were shortages of coal for heating in the winter, so we piled many layers of clothing and blankets on our beds and would even put a weighty object such as a small chair on top to try to keep warm. Some people froze to death because of the lack of heating. Electricity was only available sometimes, so we used carbide lamps that emitted a pungent smell.

Our relatives the Rechthands lived in a nearby building, and we often visited them. My paternal grandparents also lived nearby. Though they seemed reasonably well at first, my grandfather broke his hip and died of complications shortly thereafter, and my grieving grandmother contracted an illness that caused her legs to become swollen, and she followed him before too long.

~

By the summer of 1941, German businessmen were permitted to set up factories to make items such as uniforms and munitions for the German war effort. The factories employed Jewish slave labourers, who made a meagre living. The Jewish Council and various organizations set up social assistance programs to try to help the residents of the ghetto. There were soup kitchens and other social agencies. These efforts, however, were insufficient. Tremendous overcrowding created poor hygienic conditions and extreme hardship. Starvation and disease, including an epidemic of typhus transmitted by lice, claimed many thousands of lives. Corpses were lying in the streets, and I would see them being carted away for burial.

While these horrific events were taking place, some people, like my family, were better off, and life continued to go on for us in some ways. Everyone hoped that the war would end. My parents had savings, including bonds that my grandfather had willed to my mother. My father was working in the supply department of the Jewish Council, participating in the manufacturing of artificial honey from sugar, which occasionally supplemented the food rations in the ghetto. Sometimes he brought home honey for us. We were among those with some means, more so than the majority of the ghetto residents.

The German authorities moved the borders of the ghetto from

time to time, reducing the available living space, which added to our difficulties. In the autumn of 1941, the buildings on Elektoralna Street where we and the Rechthands lived were excluded from the ghetto, so we moved to a small apartment on Chłodna Street, I believe with help from Mr. Rechthand.

I spent time playing various games with my friends, including Piotr Held, the junior Jewish policeman. Although Germans forbade and closed all schools, there were secret schools, and even an underground medical school that was associated with the University of Warsaw. I've read estimations that at least five hundred students participated. There were also vocational schools that German authorities allowed. Doctors, some of whom were teaching at the medical school, researched the biological effects of starvation in the ghetto. The results were published after the war, providing important information about life and starvation in the Warsaw ghetto.

Other secret schools formed, with small groups meeting in students' apartments. I was in such a group and was taught by the professors of the Spójnia School. Professor Zdzisław Libin (Libera) taught Polish literature; Miss Ewa Tom, who was a friend of my mother's, taught biology; Professor Kojrański taught physics; and Professor Arnold Kirschbraun (Kirszbraun) taught history. I remember learning in history that the ideals of liberty and equality were mutually limiting, a tenet that I came to believe in. Girls and boys were in separate groups. I met new classmates Jerzyk Duński and Stefan Halpern. Another classmate became ill with appendicitis. His appendix burst before he could be operated on and, unfortunately, he died. His death affected me deeply. Here was a boy just like me who was no more. It was a very difficult, and personal, experience. Seeing the anonymous corpses lying on the sidewalks was certainly difficult as well, but less personal.

I spent some time with Toporol (the Society for Supporting Agriculture), a youth agency that made use of small plots of land within the ghetto to cultivate vegetables to supplement the meagre rations. We even made use of the ruins of bombed buildings, clearing away bricks and mortar before planting tomatoes and other crops in mulched earth. Participation in the activities of Toporol was thought to provide youth with agricultural training for the future, perhaps for life in Palestine, and led to positive feelings and an optimistic spirit among us. These and other activities were a form of resistance against the oppression.

Underground newspapers were printed, literary works were produced and other cultural events took place under grim conditions. There were lectures and theatrical and musical productions. More than thirty concerts and twenty recitals were put on by the Jewish Symphony Orchestra. An eleven-year-old girl played one of Mozart's piano concertos. Marysia Ajzensztadt (Eisenstadt), nicknamed the "nightingale of the ghetto," sang a number of times. In one concert I remember going to with Wanda Rechthand in 1941, one of the works played was the *Unfinished Symphony* no. 8 by Schubert. Our professor of history in the secret school played in the violin section.

There were new songs written about the realities in the ghetto; some of them set new words to pre-war tunes. Jokes, often of the black humour type, made the rounds. One was: "The last two Jews left in the ghetto meet on the street. The first asks: 'What is new?' He is told: 'Good news! The German offensive was repulsed from the gates of Washington, D.C.'"

Although thousands were starving, most were still alive, and the conditions stabilized somewhat by the summer of 1942 as the epidemic of typhus appeared to subside. But then, rumours started circulating that Jews from the Warsaw ghetto were going to be transferred eastward. Anxiety mounted. Some decided to escape the ghetto and hide in what was known as the "Aryan" part of Warsaw, including our teacher Miss Ewa Tom. She stayed overnight in our apartment on Chłodna Street before fleeing the ghetto the next morning.

∽

At this time, although we didn't know it, the Nazis were well into their "Final Solution," their plan to systematically kill all Jews in Europe. After Germany attacked the Soviet Union in June 1941 and occupied large Soviet territories, specialized Nazi troops called Einsatzgruppen were dispatched to slaughter thousands of Jews in mass shootings. At least 1.5 million people, mostly Jews but also Roma (then referred to as Gypsies) and non-Jewish communists, were murdered by Einsatzgruppen.

In December 1941, in occupied Poland, the Germans began implementing Operation Reinhard, in which Jews were first murdered by carbon monoxide gas in sealed vans in Chełmno. By March 1942, Jews were murdered in gas chambers at other death camps.

On July 22, 1942, the Germans ordered Jews to be transported out of the Warsaw ghetto. The chairman of the Jewish Council, Adam Czerniaków, died by suicide when the Germans demanded that he sign an order for the deportation of thousands of children and other inhabitants from the ghetto. Yet, transports proceeded. First the poor and homeless were taken, enticed to volunteer for the transports with offers of bread and marmalade, then the sick from the hospitals and eventually, people who could not find a valid work certificate.

Thousands of Jewish people were loaded into cattle cars at a railway siding in the northern part of the ghetto, which became known as the *Umschlagplatz* (distribution place). Germans conscripted Jewish police to bring fellow Jews to the *Umschlagplatz*, resulting in tragic situations and scenes hard to imagine. We were told that people were being moved to work in camps, but there were rumours that the truth might be worse.

Between July 22 and September 21, 1942, approximately 265,000 Jews were sent on the trains from the Warsaw ghetto. They arrived at the death camp of Treblinka, northeast from Warsaw, and were killed in the gas chambers there. Though I was very scared by what was happening around me, I was not aware of the true destination of the transports and the fate of my community.

People employed in the German factories and by the Jewish Council were at first exempted from the deportations. During those first few days, panic gripped the ghetto as crowds ran around trying to find work. I recall meeting a very disturbed friend, Andrew Lubelczyk, who was desperately trying to find a place to work so that he would be spared from a transport. Before the war, he was unusually afraid of thunderstorms and would run to hide under a bed when he would hear thunder rumble.

During that time, I was working in an office related to the Jewish Council where the vital certificates of employment were being issued, a job I likely obtained through Mr. Rechthand. Crowds of people would push against the entrance doors. It was my job to let them in a few at a time. It was difficult to stem the pressing mass of people; among the throng was a professor from my secret school.

In August, Dr. Janusz Korczak, a world-famous writer and pedagogue and principal of an orphanage in Warsaw, led all the children in his orphanage to the trains. Offered a sanctuary outside the ghetto, he refused and stayed with the children. He led them with his co-workers, some of whom were also offered refuge, in an orderly way, keeping up the children's spirits.

My father, attached to the Jewish Council's supply department, had to live near his workstation in another part of the ghetto, apart from my mother and me. I got a new job, thanks to Mr. Rechthand, who again arranged for work for me and for my mother. The job was at a German factory in the area of Smocza and Nowolipie Streets. This was a textile enterprise owned by a German businessman named Schultz. The Rechthand family was there too, with Mr. Rechthand's sister and her husband. My mother and I now lived in an apartment on Smocza Street close to the factory. Since a large proportion of the ghetto had by then been taken away, the apartments were more readily available. By then, some people had slowly begun to realize the horrible fate of the people taken away in the transports, though others did not believe it.

While we worked at the German factory, my mother became very ill, probably with dysentery. She lost a tremendous amount of weight and was just skin and bones. I tried to take care of her; the doctor who saw her recommended treatment with intravenous glucose injections. I ran through the deserted ghetto streets to a pharmacy and bought ampoules of glucose, which the doctor then administered to my mother.

An order came in the first week of September: everybody from our factory and from the other factories was to go to the *Umschlagplatz*. Not to go would be to risk death. The day was Sunday, September 6, 1942, and that day's German action was referred to as "The Cauldron." My mother was very weak and emaciated, but she bravely summoned all her strength, got dressed and put on lipstick in an attempt to look as well as possible to avoid deportation.

The sun was shining. It was a warm day. We walked together among crowds along Smocza Street toward the *Umschlagplatz*, supervised by German SS men and Jewish ghetto policemen. I heard a Jewish policeman reporting to a German SS officer, repeating, "Jawohl, Herr Commandant!" (Yes, Mister Commander!) as the German repeatedly slapped his face. We arrived at the entrance to the *Umschlagplatz*, which looked to me to be a large green field. An SS officer was motioning people to the left, toward the trains, or to the right, from where one would return to one's workplace. My mother was motioned to the left and I was motioned to the right. We looked at each other and then had to move on. I never saw my mother again.

The action of The Cauldron resulted in about fifty thousand people going to their deaths in Treblinka, some dying in the trains on the way to the camp, suffering horribly dehumanizing conditions, without food, water or basic hygienic facilities.

After the selection, I returned to where we lived near the factory. Mr. Rechthand was there, but his wife and sister-in-law had been detained at the *Umschlagplatz* with my mother. It was sometimes possible to get people back from the *Umschlagplatz* using bribes,

American dollars. Mr. Rechthand succeeded in getting his wife and sister-in-law out, but not my mother. I am sure it was not for lack of trying; my mother looked feeble from illness, and that might have made the task impossible. I was devastated and depressed. I felt hopeless, sick and unable to go to work. I begged Mr. Rechthand to issue me a certificate that I was sick so that I could stay off work. He likely had limited authority but reluctantly complied with my request. After a day or so I resumed my work duties. I struggled over the next few weeks and tried to carry on.

By the end of September, only about sixty or seventy thousand people remained in the ghetto, about half "legally" working for the German factories or for the Jewish Council and the other half staying illegally, in hiding.

At some point in early October, I received a telephone call at work. Thinking about it now, it is surprising that telephones were operating in the ghetto. But there had to be communication between the German and ghetto authorities, and certainly with the German factories. I was surprised to hear the voice of my cousin Tadzik Rosenhauch on the other end of the line. I had no idea that he was in Warsaw. How he was able to track me down, I do not know.

My cousin asked me about my mother, and I told him the sad news. My cousin and Mr. Rechthand made arrangements for me to leave the ghetto — I believe by bribing a guard — and meet Tadzik on the "Aryan" side on a specific day. My father, still in the ghetto, did not want to leave for the "Aryan" side. He was apprehensive since he had a very stereotypical Jewish appearance. He told me that a friend of his died by suicide by taking cyanide before being taken by the Germans. That was common among Jews at that time if they were able to obtain the poison. Before leaving, I walked through the empty streets of the ghetto to go say goodbye to my father in the part of the ghetto where he was staying. My father and I parted, never to see each other again.

No Longer a Child

I snuck out of the ghetto early one morning among a party of workers that was leaving the ghetto to work on the Polish side, as they did daily. We marched in formation through the ghetto gate and then through the streets outside the ghetto, which I was seeing for the first time in two years. We arrived at a carpentry workshop on Królewska Street across the street from the Saski Garden, where I had often played before the war. There appeared to be no guards, and nobody was paying attention to me. I took off my armband and slowly walked out carrying my winter coat wrapped under my arm. I proceeded, slowly and casually, along Królewska Street toward the Square of Marshal Piłsudski, which the Nazis had renamed Adolf-Hitler-Platz. There I entered a small café, the arranged meeting place. I saw my cousin Tadzik at a table with another young man whom I did not know. I walked up to them. After a casual, matter-of-fact greeting, we had a cup of tea and then left. I learned later that the other man was a member of the Polish underground and had a revolver with him for protection in case I had been followed.

My cousin first took me to a movie, so that my stereotypically Jewish face would not be seen in the streets during the day. It was dangerous for Jews with certain facial features to be seen in daylight because antisemitic Poles could recognize them as Jews. They would blackmail Jews or turn them over to the German authorities. Then we went to an apartment on Łęczycka Street in the Ochota district of the city, where Tadzik and his older brother, Zdzich, lived with a Polish family, Mrs. Zofia Herfurt and her daughter Hanka, who was nearly finished with her medical studies. They were extremely helpful to us, and I stayed there overnight.

Zdzich and Tadzik told me about how they and their parents had ended up in Warsaw. When the war broke out, my cousins and my uncle had tried to enlist with the Polish army authorities but were told to proceed eastward away from the advancing German offensive. They went toward the city of Lublin. They stopped in the town of Cyców, where many wounded Polish soldiers were trickling in from a battle that had taken place at Chełmno. My uncle and cousins attended to the wounded in a makeshift hospital, Uncle Edmund and Zdzich dressing wounds and doing surgery while Tadzik was organizing the facility and triaging the victims.

Then, as the Germans continued to advance, they had proceeded eastward to Lwów, which was under Soviet control. Zdzich worked in an eye clinic as an ophthalmologist. They were there when Germany attacked the Soviet Union and overran Lwów and Ukraine in 1941. Soon they set out northward toward the Baltic Sea, intending to get to neutral Sweden and then on to Great Britain. They got as far as the vicinity of Vilnius and found that it was too dangerous to proceed, and they returned to Lwów. As the dangers to Jews were mounting, a grateful gentile patient of Zdzich's gave him her husband's original documents, as her husband had been deported to Siberia. Tadzik obtained false "Aryan" documents, and they both went to Warsaw where they contacted friends they knew from before the war who helped them find a safe place to live and work on the "Aryan" side.

Meanwhile, my aunt and uncle had decided to go to the ghetto in Wieliczka, a town near the famous salt mines, close to Krakow. In 1942, the Germans imprisoned my uncle in the notorious prison on Montelupich Street in Krakow for close to two months. My cousins, already in Warsaw, somehow found out that he was in prison. They asked a friend, Ms. Zofia Mroszczak, to go to Krakow with a fine diamond they gave her to use as a bribe so the German officials would let my uncle go. He was released and then was in the ghetto in Krakow. He escaped by jumping from a slowly moving streetcar going around a turn near the outskirts of the ghetto. Then he and my aunt managed to flee to Warsaw, where they were now in hiding.

The next evening, Zdzich took me to another place in the suburb of Praga, on the other side of the Vistula River. We walked through the streets and over the bridge in darkness so as to avoid being noticed. I stayed with a Polish family at the apartment in Praga for some weeks. I think there were other places I was transferred to for relatively brief periods of time, though I don't recall why. The arrangements, which my cousins made for me, took a lot of effort and money and undoubtedly saved my life. The funds, I believe, came in part from the earnings of my cousins and in part from the savings their parents had from before the war.

During the time I was hiding in "Aryan" Warsaw, I had an identity document, known as a *Kennkarte*, on which was my assumed name, Janek (Jan) Warecki. My cousins obtained the false papers for me. I do not remember the official story of my assumed life. My cousins told me to learn Polish Catholic prayers and to cross myself, and I did. That was very important in case officials questioned me.

Among the places I stayed between 1942 and 1944, the longest and best time was at the apartment of Miss Zofia Różycka, who lived with her elderly mother in one of Warsaw's suburbs. I stayed with her for more than a year. Her brother, whom I met when he visited, had served as the Polish consul in New York before the war.

I stayed in a nice room and spent most of my time there. The room had a bookcase filled with the complete works of Molière translated into Polish by the talented Polish physician and poet Tadeusz Boy-Żeleński, who, I later learned, was murdered in Lwów in 1941 by a

Nazi military group together with other Polish intellectuals. I read all of Molière's works to fill the time. Because of my stereotypical Jewish appearance, I could not go out, so I stayed with Miss Różycka in her apartment. Occasionally, I met one or two neighbours who lived in the same apartment block and visited Miss Różycka.

Miss Różycka was a very kind, intelligent and understanding woman. Throughout the time I stayed with her, she would go to a lending library to get books for me to read. I also spent many good hours discussing all kinds of subjects with her and her friend Mr. Witold, who was a very bright man. He was about sixty but was in such great shape that he looked closer to forty. During that time, through my discussions and extensive reading, I became aware that for the first time in my life, I was thinking about various issues. I had stopped being a child, and I started taking stock of what had transpired and what I was able to achieve over the previous years.

During the time I was in hiding, I corresponded with my aunt Pola who also was in hiding. My cousin Tadzik served as a messenger, carrying letters back and forth. With his blond hair, he had a more non-Jewish appearance than his brother Zdzich, and it was safer for him to go outside. My aunt saved some of my letters, and I read them with some surprise more than sixty years later, having largely forgotten their content. The following English translations provide an insight into the way I lived and felt at that time.

1–4 A letter that Stefan wrote to his aunt Pola during the Holocaust, which his aunt saved throughout the war.

[undated]

Dear Auntie,

Many thanks for your letter. You are right that the most important thing now is to fill one's time, and I cope as well as I can. Recently I finished going through first-level biology, and I'm practically through physics as well. I started reading Chemistry in Daily Life, *by Lassar Cohn, which is a set of interesting lectures, as well as* The Mechanism of Human Life, *by* [George] *Dorsey, which deals with biology.*[1] *I tend to think that I would like to become a chemist, if I cannot be a general or an officer in the navy. Chemistry, apart from being quite interesting, tends to overlap and branch into two fields that I find fascinating: physics and biology. It is, if one may put it that way, very versatile. Yet my interests tend to change and are at present broad and flexible. Among the prescribed curriculum, I read through the works of* [Jan] *Kochanowski including* Satires, Trifles, Laments *and* The Dismissal of the Greek Envoys, *and now I'm reading* The Constant Prince *by* [Pedro] *Calderón* [de la Barca].

As I am bored, I intend to write an essay [titled] *"English Society in the Light of Modern Literature." I am gathering reading material, Chesterton, Smith, Huxley and Galsworthy, among others. I finished reading* Dickens *in French and now am reading* La croisière du hachich [by Henry de Monfreid]. *It is a description of adventures in Africa and the Mediterranean. Since I find it pretty difficult, with many new words, my progress is slow. I found the book by* [Pierre] *Loti biased, as he made Germans seem diabolical and the French people saintly. I read works by* [Arkady] *Fiedler, but my favourite book was* School of Eagles, *by Janusz Meissner. I recently read a book I can heartily recommend. It is one of the best books I read — Alfred Neumann's* The New Caesar, *and the second part,* Another Caesar — *an account of Napoleon III,*

---

1   A reference to either *Hows and Whys of Human Behavior* (1929) or *Why We Behave Like Human Beings* (1925) by George Dorsey.

from his birth to his death. It is excellently written and presents well the epoch of that time. The histories of the French Revolution and of the Napoleonic era are the times that I know and like the best.

Yet studying and reading cannot fill the time completely, so I have to think of other endeavours. I play various war games, imaginary sports matches, and now I make ships from tree bark, which I paint with what S. brought me [person unknown]. *A ship for you is ready, but I have not sent it, because of fear that it might get damaged in transit. It is a sort of model of* Hood [a British Royal Navy battlecruiser] *made from wooden matches. I do some simple calisthenics, as I think that one needs to do something to make up for the general lack of exercise. But the main reason is my encounter with a sixty-year-old gentleman who looks forty thanks to it. If weather permits, I sunbathe (influenced by* [Paul] *De Kruif's* Men Against Death*). Studying Latin is quite possible, but only if one does it systematically. In the first grade, when the principal taught us, I knew the subject like the back of my hand, and I was one of the best students in our class. However, afterwards I developed gaps, which I am unable to overcome. I wish for further progress. I'm not writing about S. lest he become conceited. Many kisses for Uncle. Does he remember our joke?*

Many kisses to you, Auntie,
Janek

Dear Auntie,

I received the letter and the soldiers, and I'm very grateful. The airplanes will be useful for comparison with the wooden airplanes I made, which is what I do now. I have finished manufacturing a series of three-engine "Scandinav" bombers, and now I'm switching to "Viking" light bombers.

Yes, it is sad that we can't see each other, but we shouldn't think about it or about any other current issues, because it is quite pointless. Otherwise, nothing has changed in my life. Now I'm reading The Forsyte Saga [by John Galsworthy]. S. [person unknown] says that he doesn't like such long "scrolls," unlike me. I like those that are the longest, because then one can become intimate with the heroes. I'm plodding slowly through the French book, learning about 200–250 words a month. I can read this book only very slowly, [as] it is a bit boring. I would like to read "Marie Curie" in French but it is hard to get.[2] I

---

2 Perhaps a reference to Marie Curie's thesis, Recherches sur les substances radioactives, published in 1903.

switched to making airplanes because I got bored with warships. My
fleet now has over fifty ships. I'll be signing off, I think. This letter is
short, but the time intervals are so small [niebardzo in original], *there*
isn't much to write about, because things are a bit monotonous now.
   Hugs and kisses for Uncle,
   I kiss you, Auntie,
   Janek
   PS I'm not sure if you write "nie bardzo" or "niebardzo."

~

A painful event took place during my stay with Miss Różycka. The
uprising in the ghetto erupted in April 1943. The smoke from the
burning ghetto spread over Warsaw. I knew, sadly, that my father was
likely still there, but I could not do anything about it. I never found
out what happened to him. About seven hundred and fifty mostly
young Jewish resisters decided to fight and die rather than go passive-
ly to their deaths. They fought heroically against overwhelming odds.
They had few weapons, mostly pistols, some homemade Molotov gre-
nades and a few rifles. These were procured from the "Aryan" side,
and a meagre number of small firearms were reluctantly provided by
the Polish underground forces, who refused to get involved in any
effective way in the Jewish struggle. I think that the Polish underground did not want to commit to a major intervention, thinking it
could weaken their own military actions in future.

Despite having few weapons, the Jewish ghetto fighters exacted on
the Germans unexpected setbacks and casualties. The Germans then
started burning the ghetto, building by building, and the battle ended
with the ghetto left completely in ruins. Sporadic fighting continued
for several weeks. Most of the fighters perished, including their commander, Mordecai Anielewicz. A few escaped, mostly through the
sewers to the "Aryan" side, and some survived the war in hiding or
in the partisan units in the forests. The Warsaw Ghetto Uprising was
the first organized urban resistance in Nazi-occupied Europe; other

outbreaks of resistance occurred in the Białystok ghetto and in the death camps of Treblinka, Sobibor and Auschwitz-Birkenau.

The Warsaw ghetto was no more. Few Jews remained hiding in the ghetto ruins; some might have survived. Thousands, like me, persisted in trying to endure on the "Aryan" side. When the Germans caught Jews who were hiding on the "Aryan" side of the city, they brought them to the Pawiak Prison. Over time, an estimated eight thousand Jews, as well as large numbers of Polish people, were executed in the nearby ruins of the ghetto.

~

One day in early 1944, two Polish policemen arrived, came into my room early in the morning and said that I should get dressed and go with them to the police precinct. I was terribly scared, and I pleaded with them, saying I was sick. They told me to drop my pyjama trousers. I murmured something like "Oh, is that what this is all about?" and lowered my pants. They looked and, without saying much, left! Undoubtedly my life was saved because my father had refused to allow me to be circumcised when I was born, perhaps because of concern for my pain or for aesthetic considerations. It became obvious that one of Miss Różycka's neighbours had informed the police, and so it was not safe for me to stay with her any longer.

Miss Różycka notified my cousin Tadzik. He and his family made arrangements, and he soon arrived and took me to a clinic. There, under local anesthetic, a specialist operated on my curved nose and made it straight. I learned after the war that surgeons were performing plastic surgery not only on faces but also on penises, to restore foreskin, thus making it easier for Jews to pass as "Aryans" and hopefully improve their chances of survival. After a few days, when the bruising around my nose subsided, I left the clinic. My cousins found a room for me with a Polish family who did not know that I was Jewish. For the first time since leaving the ghetto, I was able to move about freely and appeared to live the life of a Polish youth in Warsaw.

I always felt some anxiety that I might get caught or exposed, but I was able to deal with it and maintained a relaxed, matter-of-fact air about me that was essential.

One day, while walking down a wide street, I saw walking toward me a young Jewish girl who had been one of my peers from before the war, Ela Fishaut. We stopped, at first awkwardly, and said hello and talked for a few minutes. She told me where she lived with her mother, Mrs. Helena Fishaut, who had run the private group school and summer camps before the war, and invited me to visit. I did, and we talked, particularly about people we knew.

I believe it was from this visit that I learned that Wanda Rechthand, the bright young daughter of Mr. Rechthand, who was of so much help to my family and me, had managed to leave the ghetto and had been living on the "Aryan" side. Another of the young girls we knew also wanted to leave the ghetto, and the Rechthands helped her leave. Unfortunately, she and Wanda were both caught and had not been heard from since; most likely they were executed near the Pawiak Prison in the ghetto. When I mentioned to my cousins my encounter and visit with the Fishauts, they said that it was potentially dangerous and that I was not to contact them again. Indeed, I did not even see my cousins often because of the danger to all of us.

The Tide of War

By the summer of 1944, the tide of war had turned. The German army, which in 1941 and 1942 had reached deep into Soviet territory, was retreating, and the advancing Soviet army arrived not far from Warsaw. Late in the afternoon of August 1, I was walking home and by chance met my cousin Zdzich. He was still living and hiding at the Herfurts, the same apartment in which I had stayed the first night after leaving the ghetto. I lived in the same district not far from the Narutowicz Square. There seemed to be some excitement in the air. We parted and I went home. Soon the news spread that the Polish underground, the Home Army (Armia Krajowa or AK), had started an uprising and was taking control of Warsaw from the German army.

The political situation, and perhaps the historical Polish fighting tradition, led to the decision of the Home Army to stage the uprising. Fighters in the Warsaw Uprising managed to liberate about a hundred and twenty Jews, as well as Polish inmates, from the prison and concentration camp established by the Germans on Gęsia Street in October 1943. After regaining their freedom, some of the inmates joined the struggle against the Germans and fought with distinction.

The uprising lasted until October 2, when the Polish command surrendered. Approximately 25 per cent of Warsaw was destroyed during the uprising and more than one hundred and fifty thousand civilians, including Jews, died in the uprising. The large loss of life was in vain — the uprising failed. The Soviet army had offered little to no help. A detachment of Polish soldiers who fought with the Soviet army temporarily crossed the Vistula River and connected briefly with the insurgents but could not hold their positions. Politics were involved in the power play between the Soviets and the Home Army, which was loyal to the Polish government-in-exile in London. Allied airplanes, which flew over Warsaw from far away fields in Western Europe, attempted to help the Polish forces by dropping weapons and supplies. The task was very difficult, because the Soviets refused to allow them to land in the territories that they controlled nearby. The Allied planes, some of which were flown by Canadian pilots — were sometimes shot down by German forces.

The uprising in 1944, combined with the 1939 siege of the city, resulted in the near complete destruction of beautiful Warsaw. Included in the destruction was the infamous Pawiak Prison, which stood within the ghetto borders.

During the first few days of the uprising, the family I was staying with and I were holed up indoors while the noise of gunfire and explosions were raging outside. Soon the German army took control of the outlying parts of Warsaw, including the area where we were. They ordered everybody out, set each building on fire, and had us walk out of the city. As I walked among crowds through the fields outside of Warsaw, members of Lithuanian or other Baltic and Ukrainian army units fighting with the Germans guarded us. They stopped people and took away any valuables they might have had. One young soldier stopped and searched me. He found a gold watch given to me by my mother that had belonged to my grandfather and a ring with a small diamond. He took the watch and to my surprise gave the ring back, saying, "This for me, and this for you."

We eventually arrived in a maintenance yard for locomotives in the village of Pruszków, where a transit camp had been formed for the thousands who had walked from Warsaw. From there, people were either sent by trains to Germany to work for the German war effort, or were transported to the Nazi camps as political prisoners. I met Miss Różycka and her friend Witold briefly in the Pruszków camp. I almost went on a train with them, but the guards stopped me before I was able to follow, presumably because the train was full. In the camp in Pruszków, there were Polish medics and doctors from a nearby hospital in the village of Tworki, and they tried to get young Polish men out of the camp by claiming they had dysentery. I was among these young men, and after a few days in the hospital, I was released and freed.

Soon after my release, however, I was on a local train when it was stopped and all passengers were told to get out and stand in line. An officer in a German uniform inspected us. He spoke fluent Polish; he was likely a *Volksdeutscher*, an ethnic German who lived in Poland before the war. He said to me, "You look Jewish!" Amazingly, I answered flippantly and responded that perhaps my great-grandmother had a soft spot in her heart for a Jew. The officer then just passed on down the line, and I was brought back to the Pruszków camp. My casual response likely saved me from serious danger. How was it that I, an inexperienced teenager, who tended to be overprotected at home and did not have street smarts, acted so coolly?

Now knowing the ropes in the camp, I pretended to get dysentery again and was admitted to the Tworki hospital and released again. This time, the Polish staff assigned me to a Polish farmer in the countryside, in a village in the area of Łowicz. I stayed there and lived with a family of local farmers. I used my mother's ring to buy a warm coat for the winter. I slept on a bunk in a stable that I shared with a horse and attended church on Sundays with the whole community. This was the obligatory social highlight of life in the rural areas. The villagers were simple, poor people who were somewhat reluctant to share their limited resources with the strangers from Warsaw. They had no choice, however, since the official head of the area issued specific orders in this regard. During the meals, everybody ate together from one big bowl using individual spoons. I felt awkward among these country people. I also felt very isolated and alone. I wondered what had happened to my cousins, aunt and uncle. I remembered that my mother had spoken — probably when we were in the ghetto — of her cousin Adam Pragier, who, at the outbreak of the war, was in France and then escaped to London, where he was a member of the Polish government-in-exile. I thought that if I could somehow manage to get to Western Europe, I could contact him. It was just a pipe dream, however, as there was no practical way that I could accomplish it. I just continued to hang on, and eventually the Soviet offensive reached and passed the area in 1945.

~

Finally, the war was coming to an end. The Allied armies had landed in Europe and opened western fronts, first in Italy and then in France. The German forces were unable to resist the offensives from the west, and the Soviet armies were advancing from the east. The American and British air forces' planes were bombing German cities and factories. Liberation of Europe from Hitler's hordes was taking place, and in May 1945, Germany surrendered. Tragically, for the majority of European Jewry, the end came too late.

Between 1941 and the end of the war, about six million Jewish people from German-occupied Europe were murdered — gassed in the death camps of Treblinka, Chelmno, Belzec, Sobibor, Majdanek and Auschwitz-Birkenau; killed with machine guns by the hundreds of thousands by the Einsatzgruppen in Ukraine and the Soviet Union; died from starvation, violence, overwork or disease in concentration camps or forced labour camps; were individually shot when caught in hiding; and were killed during death marches, when thousands of camp prisoners were mercilessly driven by their German tormentors westward as the Soviet armies were approaching the camps, threatening to encircle them.

Yet, a small fraction of the Jewish people in Europe survived despite the Nazis' attempts to destroy them. Like me, many survived in hiding, often helped by those who became known as righteous gentiles. Others survived after fleeing occupied areas or being taken east by the Soviets, returning after the war ended. And some managed to stay alive in the camps, or in hiding or fighting as partisans in the forests of Poland, Lithuania and Belarus, participating in resistance and sabotaging the German war effort.

In the Aftermath

After the Soviet armies moved westward toward Berlin, my life quieted down somewhat. Crowds of displaced people started travelling on foot or by bicycle or in overcrowded, irregularly running trains, from wherever they were at the end of the hostilities. They tried to return home, although their homes often did not exist, or to find family, or at least to register with various aid organizations to help them search.

Although it was known that Warsaw was almost completely destroyed, many people set out toward it, and so did I. I knew that I had lost my parents, but I did not know what had happened to my relatives. I was hoping that I might be able to find my cousins Tadzik and Zdzich and their parents, who I knew had been in Warsaw at least until the uprising in the autumn of 1944.

I first stopped at the hospital in Tworki, where I had stayed before being sent to the countryside. I met some nurses who knew me, and they said that the new chief physician wanted to see me. When I entered his office, he said that he knew my aunt Pola and uncle Edmund and that they were looking for me! He gave me their address in Krakow. I took a train to Katowice and then went on to Krakow.

I walked through the streets of that beautiful city with its medieval architecture and many churches. It looked the way I remembered it from our visits there before the war, untouched by the ravages of Hitler's army. I made my way to the address I had been given, an apartment building on Dunajewskiego Street no. 3. I walked up the stairs, located the apartment number and rang the bell. The door opened, and there was my aunt Pola in a black dress. She opened her arms with an exclamation of relief and joy, and we embraced. Then my uncle appeared. I was with my family again. The reunion, however, was not completely joyous. I learned that my wonderful cousin Tadzik had been killed during the Warsaw Uprising in 1944.

Tadzik had volunteered as a medic in a hospital associated with the Polish underground, which staged the uprising, together with his gentile girlfriend, Danuta Krzeszewska. The hospital, run by the Order of the Knights of Malta, was an active military hospital throughout the war, and members of the Polish underground were hidden and secretly treated there, but its activities were especially important during the uprising. Its director was lieutenant and doctor Stanisław Milewski-Lipkowski. A letter that he wrote to my aunt Pola informed her of my cousin's fate and gave some insight into the horrific events that the medics lived through.

Dr. Milewski-Lipkowski wrote to my aunt that he had immediately developed "a sympathetic and mutually trusting relationship" with my cousin, whose alias was Doctor Graszewski, and that he "went to work with enthusiasm and continued effort, which within a couple of hours won the appreciation of all the personnel." He also wrote that he would inform my cousin's high school in Krakow of his efforts because they should be proud of their graduate.

His letter to my aunt was long, discussing the German offensive on August 7, when the German burned buildings on Elektoralna Street. This was where my grandparents lived before and during the war and where I stayed for a period of time in the ghetto. In an attack from the Saski Garden, Dr. Milewski-Lipkowski related that he was severely wounded in an attack, and the hospital was eventually overtaken by the Germans on August 14 by a group of a hundred and fifty vicious and drunken SS men, who forced everyone to leave immediately. By a quirk of fate, the hospital staff was able to relocate to a nearby part of the city centre still held by the Polish insurgents. The doctor wrote more details in the letter, excerpted here:

The state of my health was quite precarious and I had surgery. During that time, I saw Doctor Graszewski (as I always thought of him) only a few times when he visited me. I heard many praises and words of appreciation and sympathy from people who worked with him. On the 4th of September there began a steady barrage of artillery, together with aerial bombing, which within a number of hours destroyed the city centre. In the morning, around nine or ten o'clock, the building at Jasna Streeet 11 was hit badly. Dr. Graszewski was wounded lightly in the head. He dressed the wound and with Sister Krzeszewska they began to move the wounded and other patients from the bombed building to the neighbouring house…. Dr. Graszewski and Sister Krzeszewska were carrying a wounded woman [Janina Sarnecka, a sister of Hanka Herfurt]. *All three were killed by a single missile. At the same time, my quarters were bombed…. During these two hours, nine members of our staff perished and I do not know how many patients. Taking advantage of another lull in the attacks I managed to get to where the* [staff and patients] *of our hospital were camped out on the staircase. Those that were not wounded or injured were in shock. In the courtyard, covered with blankets, lay the remains of Dr. Graszewski. I took leave of him with a short prayer. I said goodbye to a young patriot, a noble man who perished at his post while rescuing a compatriot. I envied him then, that fate let him perish nobly and spared him living through the indignity of defeat and ill treatment. He died as a free man while performing the most admirable Samaritan mission of love of his fellow being.*

My depiction above might be somewhat too brutal. Yet, it is difficult to relate the events of the uprising without a modicum of reality, which was nightmarish. That is why one cannot assess human character within hours, days or weeks. A few moments encompassed whole epochs and revealed the true value of the human character. One saw people without masks and that is why, although our collaboration was brief, I do not hesitate to declare that I came to know Dr. Graszewski the way he was to the core — a shining spirit. I am certain that if he had survived the uprising, we would have been bound by a lasting friendship. Alas, Fate ordained otherwise.

My aunt and uncle knew Tadzik's girlfriend, Danuta, and her mother, Florentyna; they had met before the war while skiing during winter vacations. They helped my relatives to survive while in the city and greater area of Warsaw. Danuta knew four languages and studied philosophy before the war and then in secret during the war. During the Siege of Warsaw in 1939, she helped move the archives of the University of Warsaw from a burning building. She was wounded and was awarded the Cross of Valour. Today, Tadzik's and Danuta's names are inscribed on the memorial wall of the Warsaw Rising Museum, which commemorates the city uprising.

I was very sad to hear this news about my cousin, and obviously my aunt and uncle were affected very deeply. I felt somewhat guilty that I survived, while Tadzik, whom I loved so much and without whose care I would not have survived, did not. However, my aunt and uncle welcomed me with love, and it was clear that I was now a member of their immediate family. Still, I tended at times to think that it was all a mistake and that Tadzik might one day appear. We didn't know what had happened to my cousin Zdzich, but it seemed likely that he had been taken from Warsaw in 1944 for forced labour in Germany. We were hoping that we would hear from him as time went on.

My aunt and uncle told me more about their tribulations during the war. My uncle was imprisoned but then released. While imprisoned, he was ordered to take care of an eye problem of a high-ranking German official. It is possible it was that official who was bribed for his release. Through the assistance of Florentyna and Danuta Krzeszewska, my aunt and uncle were hidden in Warsaw and in its vicinity, at one point sheltered in a convent in Chotomów. They had many close calls and were blackmailed by unscrupulous Poles, but they were also greatly helped by righteous Poles.

~

I stayed with Aunt Pola and Uncle Edmund and would often visit our neighbour, Mrs. Bonhard. She had lost her husband during the war and was crestfallen. She played piano well, and I would listen to her play Beethoven's piano sonatas. The music had a soothing effect. Perhaps I felt a connection to the past and my mother's music making.

My aunt went to Warsaw to bring Tadzik's remains back to Krakow, accompanied by Mr. Józef, a faithful driver of my uncle and aunt before and during the war. She returned with my cousin's remains and he was buried with a brief funeral ceremony in a Jewish cemetery in a suburb of Krakow.

It was from my aunt that I acquired some family photographs from before the war. When my aunt and uncle had returned to Krakow shortly after the war, they went to their previous home, which was now in the hands of the Soviet army officials. My aunt and uncle were allowed to take some of their belongings that were still there, which was unusual. Strangely, along with the photographs, the officials told them to take their set of the famous Rosenthal china; apparently, the difference from their name of Rosenhauch was not noticed, because the officials said that it must obviously be theirs as it was marked with their name!

I did not know what had happened to other members of my family: the Centnerszwers, or my cousins Janek and Ryś. I never found out what happened to my uncle Władek Reicher or great-aunts Leonka and Gutka; presumably they perished. Much later, I learned that Uncle Maks and Aunt Stasia had been in the city of Białystok during the war, which was, until 1941, in the territories occupied by the Soviet Union. They were killed in the Białystok ghetto in 1943.

Somehow, I learned that some of my peers from before the war did survive. Agencies or various organizations — Polish, Jewish and others set up by the Red Cross — had appeared over the weeks and months that followed the liberation in larger centres so family members and friends could establish contact. I corresponded with Alinka Puszet who lived in Katowice; she married and moved to Warsaw and lived on Elektoralna Street. She later immigrated to Israel. Ela Fishaut settled in Australia after getting married and Hanka Kon married a gentile and remained in Poland. My bright friend Stefan Kraushar, who wrote to the president of Poland before the war, survived and settled in the United States. Jaś Ramberg, my friend and son of the principal of our Spójnia School, immigrated to Israel where he became a brilliant scientist.

Among those who did not survive was Staś (Stanisław) Kopel with whom I played in Warsaw during the early period of occupation, before the formation of the ghetto. Mr. Rechthand and his beautiful older daughter, Genia, also did not survive — they were caught and killed on the "Aryan" side just a few days before Warsaw was liberated in 1945. Of that family, only Mrs. Rechthand was to survive the war. There is a grave for Mr. Rechthand and his two daughters, Wanda and Genia, in the Okopowa Street Jewish Cemetery in Warsaw.

Although many of us felt elated that we survived, we also grieved the deaths of our friends and families. So many of us did not know what had happened to our dear ones and kept wandering in search of them.

Many people were apprehensive and uncertain of what the future held, since the communities where they had lived before the war had been completely destroyed. This insecurity was reinforced to a considerable degree by the rise of virulent antisemitism and the outbreak of anti-Jewish violence in the country. Between liberation and the beginning of 1947, hundreds of Jews were murdered by Poles. Included in that number were those killed in large pogroms in villages, in cities — most notably in Kielce — and in forests by the armed Polish detachments of the Narodowe Siły Zbrojne (National Armed Forces).

I slowly settled into our life in the beautiful city of Krakow with its many medieval buildings. There was the magnificent Wawel castle of the Polish kings. There was a ribbon of parkland called Planty encircling the central part of the city, replacing the walls and moat that had defended the city in the remote past. And in the main market square of the city was St. Mary's Basilica, where a trumpeter played part of a tune known as *hejnał mariacki* daily on the hour, commemorating a legend from the past.

I enrolled in an accelerated high school course intended to allow students to complete two years in one to make up for the time lost during the war. I was taking the last two high school years in 1945–1946, enjoying biology and other subjects. I found that I was able to write compositions better than before the war, perhaps because of the extensive reading I did while hiding in the apartment of Miss Różycka in Warsaw.

My uncle was practising ophthalmology in an office attached to the apartment where we lived. He allowed me to watch him and at times to assist in a minor way, and he would explain his findings and the treatments he was using. As a result of this experience, I gradually grew interested in medicine and decided that I would like to study it after finishing high school. Hanka Herfurt, who with her mother, Zofia, helped my cousins by hiding them during the war, was also in Krakow. She was continuing with her medical studies and assisted my uncle during surgery.

During this time, we officially changed our last name. We felt that we did not want to bear names of German derivation. Carter was the last name of my beloved cousin Tadzik's favourite character in a book — detective Nick Carter — and so we adopted it.

At some point, we found out that my cousin Janek, the older son of my aunt Karola, had died shortly after the war, and that my cousin Ryś had survived by escaping to England. But by late 1945 or early 1946, we still hadn't heard anything about Zdzich. My aunt, a very determined person, set out courageously on her own to Germany to look for him. We finally heard from my aunt that she had found my cousin Zdzich, who was working as a physician in the displaced persons (DP) camp in Landsberg, Germany. My aunt and cousin soon moved to Munich. We planned to join them there, but before leaving, I hoped to pass a hastily arranged examination to get my final high school diploma in the spring of 1946. This was done with the kind cooperation of the Polish school authorities, since the final school year was not yet completed. I had to cram for the examination, including material for the course Introduction to Philosophy, which I had not yet begun! Fortunately, I was able to pass and obtain the certificate.

My uncle had official permission to travel abroad and went from Krakow to Prague, the capital of Czechoslovakia. I did not have this permission, so he arranged for me to travel illegally, which meant that after a train ride to a town near the border of Czechoslovakia, I had to proceed to a certain house, where I gave a password and was let in. That night, the guides took me — actually carried me on their backs — across a river to a town on the other side of the border, where I waited for a couple of days for a document that allowed me to take a train to Prague. I met my uncle there and we spent three days in that beautiful city and then left for Germany, arriving by train to Munich.

My cousin Zdzich told me a bit about his experiences, and about the horrendous conditions Jews experienced right after the war. Zdzich had been liberated by the Americans and worked with a US Air Force unit as an interpreter. One day, two Jewish GIs came to talk to him. They were concerned about Jews in the recently liberated camps of Dachau and Buchenwald, who were continuing to die at a high rate because of the lack of adequate food supplies and medical care. The soldiers wrote letters to US authorities detailing the gross negligence, and their determined efforts eventually led to an investigation and an intervention by President Truman.[1]

---

1   Robert Hilliard was one of the two American soldiers who had talked to my cousin, and he discusses this story in his book *Surviving the Americans: The Continued Struggle of the Jews After Liberation*.

Now, Zdzich was working as a physician at the UNRRA (United Nations Relief and Rehabilitation Administration) University for displaced persons in Munich. The university occupied the building complex of the Deutsches (German) Museum on an island on the Isar River in the centre of the city, where the students and staff lived and studied. I shared a room with Zdzich. The university was bustling with activity and people from virtually all countries of Eastern and Central Europe.

I enrolled in a pre-medical course consisting of various biological sciences and remember well the lectures of Professor Novikov, who had taught at the Moscow State University and other institutions in Berlin and Prague and was an impressive lecturer. I interacted with students of many nations and detected only occasionally antisemitic attitudes. Since the end of the war, because of the horrific experiences that we had to go through because of intolerance and hatred, I reasoned idealistically, and perhaps naively, that I must strive to be different, and I decided to base my relationship with others on what they were like as individuals and not on their ethnic origin.

Displaced people in Germany realized the temporary nature of their situation and tried to make plans for emigration. At one point, Zdzich and I took a few Spanish lessons, as there was a possibility of emigration to South America. Meanwhile, my uncle and aunt established contact with his sister who lived in New York City. Eventually, it was possible for her to make arrangements for my uncle, aunt and Zdzich to go to the United States. Unfortunately, I could not be included because of the restrictive immigration laws; I was not technically a member of the immediate family. This caused my family considerable worry until a solution presented itself.

When my cousin Zdzich was working in the DP camp in Landsberg he met a Jewish nurse from Canada, Etta Brenner, who also worked for the UNRRA. She was originally from Warsaw but had immigrated to Canada to join her uncle and aunt, Volodia and Mary Kitzes, many years before the war. Etta contacted her family and they agreed to sponsor me to come to Winnipeg, as part of a new measure to allow immigration of displaced people. I learned much later that it was a part of a brand-new Canadian policy on immigration and that previously Canada had a very restrictive policy that prevented most Jewish and many other immigrants from entering the country.

The immigration process was very, very slow. In the meantime, my uncle became the physician-in-chief of a DP camp in Feldafing, a town on the beautiful Lake Würm (now called Starnberg), a short train ride from Munich. I visited my uncle and aunt there often and spent pleasant times with them. One day, I saw my friend Stefan Halpern from the secret school in the Warsaw ghetto walk up the steps of the Deutsches Museum in Munich. We renewed our friendship, and he came to visit me a few times in Feldafing. He later enrolled at a university in Frankfurt am Main. I visited him once in Frankfurt where we went to see the opera *Martha* (known popularly as *Faust*) by Gounod. Stefan later immigrated to the United States and settled in Los Angeles, where he worked as a psychologist.

In Munich, besides studying, I took swimming lessons, watched famous marionettes at the Marienplatz New Town Hall do a daily dance to music, and attended operas and concerts. The price of tickets was quite affordable, compared to the high prices of many food items, which were also difficult to obtain. One of the concerts was most remarkable. The young Yehudi Menuhin, who was Jewish, performed with a German orchestra. Some Jewish people were shocked that he would do that. He played the violin concertos by Bach, Mendelssohn and Beethoven, and for the encore played the "Chaconne for Solo Violin" by Bach. Seated near me were German students who were beside themselves marvelling at his playing. I felt a reawakening of my interest in music and took a few lessons in music theory from a German teacher for which I paid with tins of sardines. Whatever I learned, however, was not applied and was soon forgotten.

There was a Jewish Students' Union where I met many friends, some of whom I was to become reacquainted with in Winnipeg.

Among the students I met was Adam Rosenblum. We were both studying medicine and attended lectures together. Adam was a short man with greying hair, older than my peers and me. He told me that he was a pharmacist in Warsaw before the war, was in the Polish army in 1939, and was taken by the Germans as a prisoner of war. We shared an interest in music and attended concerts together frequently.

After a year or so, the UNRRA and its university were dissolved, and I transferred to another university in the city. I continued with my studies and made new friends, and I once attended a special meeting organized by a Jewish student who was in a Zionist movement that endeavoured to bring as many Jews as possible to Palestine. He wanted us all to commit then and there and sign up for immigration to Palestine. I had my plans with my family and so did other students, so he failed to persuade most of us. After he left for Palestine, he, along with many others, was caught by the British and interned in Cyprus.

As I continued studying in Munich and going through the unending immigration process, my family left for the United States. I was slowly studying English. After going through a book of English grammar, I started reading the novel *Earth and High Heaven* by Canadian author Gwethalyn Graham. Published in 1944, it was the first Canadian novel to reach number one on the *New York Times* bestseller list. I wrote down innumerable new words and memorized their meanings.

Eventually, I was able to establish contact with my cousin Ryś in England. When the war began in 1939, Ryś had been studying in Switzerland, but he was very patriotic, and he set out for Poland through the Balkans to help fight Poland's enemies. He arrived in Lwów, where he joined the army in defending the city. When the Soviet troops overcame the Polish forces, Ryś was taken prisoner. He escaped and was able to make his way through the border to Hungary and then on to France. He left for England on the last ship from France as the German army overran the country. In July 1940, he joined the 1st Polish Armoured Division in England and fought in France,

Belgium and the Netherlands. After the war, he settled in England, as did a number of Polish soldiers. He married a young British woman named Doris. I exchanged letters with them, and Doris gracefully referred to my newly learned English as "charming."

The immigration offices were situated some distance from the city of Munich, so prospective immigrants had to take lengthy train rides to the Funk Caserne, previously the military barracks, where immigration and health officials filled out many forms and performed medical examinations.

Finally, toward the end of the summer of 1948, all the formalities were completed, and I was cleared to proceed to Bremerhaven, from where ships were taking immigrants to North America. Before I left, my friend Adam Rosenblum gave me a musical composition of his, under the pen name E. Leves, to take with me for safekeeping, as he was remaining to continue his studies in Munich.

The officials in Bremerhaven were looking for people who could help perform various tasks on the ship. I applied to be an interpreter and was accepted. Our ship was an army transport, the *General Stuart Heintzelman*. The September journey was very pleasant except for the first day, when in choppy waters of the English Channel, many of us became seasick and were "feeding the fish." The weather turned calmer. I saw flying fish from the deck of the ship. After some eight days at sea, I arrived at Pier 21 in Halifax and went through the Canadian immigration process.

Soon I boarded a train and travelled for a couple of days. Early on, the train went through Quebec. When it stopped, I tried to buy food, and had great difficulty in communicating with the locals. Although I knew French well enough to communicate, they either did not understand my pronunciation or pretended not to understand. The train then sped for hours through a beautiful world of lakes and forests. I looked at it with wonder, thinking how much I would love to explore such a land in the future.

Learning Experiences

Eventually I arrived in Winnipeg and disembarked at Union Station. In the crowd at the railway station, I recognized Etta, who introduced me to her uncle Volodia and aunt Mary. We drove to their home, my new home, at 657 St. Matthews Avenue, a house that incorporated the grocery store that Volodia and Mary Kitzes ran.

I shared a room with their son Ben, a young man who worked as a pharmacist. During the war, he had served in the Canadian Air Force. He soon introduced me to the Canadian Football League. He was an avid fan of the Winnipeg Blue Bombers and took me to a game at the Osborne Stadium. I sat and watched, considerably confused. I saw two teams in colourful uniforms lined up against each other. After the referee's whistle, a pile-up of players immediately resulted, and so it went, apart from an occasional kick of the funny-shaped ball down the field! This was very different from European football, called soccer in North America.

The Kitzes family made me feel at home and essentially became my adopted family. I helped Volodia in the evenings to square his daily store accounts. He was a gentle, easygoing man who was interested in the opera. Volodia came from Odessa and had met Mary in France. They married and came to Canada before World War I. After the war began, they remained and became Canadian citizens. Mary was born in Puławy, a town in Poland. Auntie Mary, as I called her, was a woman with a strong personality, the leader of the family. She held strong opinions and did not hesitate to express them.

Ben worked in a drugstore that he co-owned at Corydon Avenue and Wilton Street. Ben had a car, and I learned how to drive and worked delivering for the drugstore. The streets south of Corydon were not paved, and if it started raining, I had to hurry so I could get out before the streets became muddy and impassable.

Ben's younger sister, Juliette, was married to Marcel Goldenberg and lived in New York, where they were friendly with my family there. Volodia had other relatives who lived in New York and its surrounding area. A few months after my arrival, Juliette and Marcel came for a visit with their baby daughter, Diane.

I corresponded with a few friends in Europe but primarily, I was absorbed in my new environment and life in Winnipeg. I attended a concert of the Winnipeg Symphony Orchestra directed by its first conductor, Walter Kaufmann. They performed Handel's *Messiah*, which I had not previously heard. I was enchanted with the beauty of the music and the wonderful aria-like solos.

I met many friends of the Kitzes family. Among their closest friends was the Werier family; Mania was the mother's name and I recall four of her six children. Val was a journalist working then for the *Winnipeg Tribune*, and his very charming fiancée was named Eva. When I attended their wedding, it was the first time in my life that I saw a chuppah. Val's brother George was an actor, Harry a social worker, and their sister Ruth was a pianist.

Prior to coming to Canada, I had corresponded with Rabbi Milgrom of Hillel and the Jewish Federation of Winnipeg about continuing my studies. Soon after I arrived in September 1948, Rabbi Milgrom drove me to the campus of the University of Manitoba. I registered for the second year of the pre-medical course. I met many classmates — Jewish and non-Jewish Canadians from Winnipeg, from rural Manitoba and Saskatchewan, and some Canadian and British war veterans who were older than me. I was familiar with some of the courses from my studies in Munich: physics, chemistry, botany and zoology. I also took introductory French, which was easy for me because of my studies in Poland, and English, which was the biggest hurdle. I studied hard. In the English course we took Chaucer, Milton, Johnson and Wordsworth. At the end of the year, my lowest mark of 67 per cent in English was also the mark I was most proud of. I had high marks in other subjects and won an Isbister Scholarship for one of the highest standings, which would prove helpful when I applied for admission into medicine the following year.

I could not visit my family in New York until I became a Canadian citizen, which would take five years, or I would risk not being let back into Canada. So, I corresponded with them in writing and by telephone. My uncle was allowed to practice ophthalmology after passing only an English language test. He was not required to take medical examinations because of his renown. My cousin Zdzich, who started using his middle name George (Jerzy), also pursued a career in ophthalmology.

I also corresponded with my cousin Ryś in London, where he ran a business; with one or two of my friends in Poland; and with my friend Adam Rosenblum in Munich. He remained there and finished his medical studies. In 1951, he came to Canada and wrote to me from Montreal. He had come on a contract to work as a chemist in a chemical factory, but this turned out to be a spurious formality. In reality, he was given work in a hospital, as an orderly and in the kitchen. After a few weeks he was given work as a laboratory assistant, but he was very underpaid. Adam's letters to me in 1952 made it clear that he was extremely unhappy with the conditions in which he found himself in Montreal. He had to work for low wages doing chores that were not related to his qualifications, and he did not see any realistic prospects for improvement. He felt that he could not stand the situation much longer and wrote that he was saving in order to return to Germany or even to Poland. Then I never heard from him again.

Through some connections from my family in New York, I got work at a firm during the Christmas vacations, helping with the Christmas season mail. There, I met and worked together with another young boy from Europe, John Hirsch. John, a Holocaust survivor from Hungary, had come to Winnipeg with a group of Jewish orphans a year before I did. John was a brilliant student. He studied English literature and was interested in theatre. He went on to found the Manitoba Theatre Centre (MTC, now the Royal MTC) and became a world-famous theatre director. Our paths were to cross again a few years later.

I spent the summers of 1949 and 1950 working as a member of a travelling X-ray unit that did chest X-rays throughout the province of Manitoba. This was a part of a tuberculosis prevention program. The units were big trucks with X-ray machines under the direction of an X-ray technician-driver and two student assistants. We X-rayed hundreds of people in towns all over the province, from north of Winnipeg to the towns in the south near the border with the US, and from the western towns such as Melita and St. Lazare, which was situated in a beautiful valley, to the eastern regions near western Ontario. St. Lazare and Sainte Rose du Lac were towns with a French-speaking population, and other towns were filled with people of Icelandic origins. My nondescript accent made it difficult for people to tell my origins and I was taken for a European from many different countries. We stayed in the local hotels during the weekdays and usually returned to Winnipeg for weekends, and I got to know Manitoba well.

During an early trip, I became acquainted with a North American dish that was new to me. We stopped at a roadside food stand and ordered a "nip" — what Manitobans seemed to call a hamburger. One of my fellow students was Hal, who was German, and that put my resolve to be tolerant to the test, but we got along well. My other fellow student was Maurice, a young French-Canadian, who was later a broadcaster on the local French radio station CKSB.

During one of these summers, an unusual incident occurred. One evening, our X-ray technician suddenly started running around wildly. He indicated that an insect had gotten into his ear and was buzzing loudly, driving him crazy. I obtained small tweezers from somebody and, using my knowledge of the anatomy of the ear canal,

I was able to remove the bee. The technician reminded me more than fifty years later that he had been my first patient!

~

With positive references I managed to acquire through Etta, and with my Isbister Scholarship, my chances for admission into medicine were good, and I succeeded in getting into first-year medicine in the fall of 1949.

I felt awe when I first walked the hallowed halls of the medical faculty buildings. Our class of 1954 totalled about seventy students, six of them women. I knew most of my classmates from the previous year at the university; our group had varied backgrounds, but I was the only student from Continental Europe. They were mostly Canadians from Manitoba or Saskatchewan. Among them was Hiro Nishioka of Japanese heritage. His family, who resided in British Columbia, had been dispossessed and forcibly relocated during World War II because they were unjustly considered as potentially dangerous "foreign aliens" after Japan attacked the United States. Hiro took lecture notes in so small and meticulous a handwriting that he could practically fit a whole course content on the back of a postcard! Not surprisingly, he became a neurosurgeon. Among my Canadian colleagues were a large number of Jewish-Canadians. That was a huge change from just a few years earlier, when there were admission quotas for students of Jewish origin and others.

I did not learn the details of what actually transpired to bring that change about until more than half a century later, when my classmate Dr. Morris Loffman gave a talk at the fiftieth reunion of our class in 2004.[1] I had heard about antisemitism in Manitoba, as in other

---

1 The issue was also written about in an essay on antisemitism in Manitoba by Jonathan Fine of Kelvin High School, which won the Manitoba Historical Society's 1995 Dr. Edward C. Shaw Young Historians Award and by the journalist Terence Moore in articles in the journal *Manitoba Medicine* in 1988 and 1989. For references on this issue, see the appendix.

parts of Canada, between the 1940s and the 1960s, when Jews were not welcomed at some recreational clubs. In 1948, this was perhaps unofficial policy at Winnipeg's own Puffin Ski Club. That same year, newspapers in Winnipeg reported that a middle-class residential development, Wildwood Park, as well as the upper-class exclusive neighbourhood of Tuxedo, excluded Jews. Jews were also restricted from owning or renting properties at Victoria Beach, a popular summer retreat for gentiles. Some of the Jewish orphans who came to Winnipeg during the same period as me encountered prejudice when they were not accepted for jobs after writing "Jewish" as their cultural origin on applications.

However, it was the antisemitism at the Faculty of Medicine at the University of Manitoba, which had been operating under a secret quota system in the 1930s and 1940s, that I was most interested in. When I learned about this history in Canada, I was reminded of the quotas limiting admission of Jewish students in Poland before World War II, and of the "ghetto benches," which my cousin Tadzik experienced in Krakow.

Dr. Alvin T. Mathers, Dean of Medicine, had supported this discriminatory admissions practice. In 1943, a Jewish student group, the Avukah Society, began researching the issue and compiling data. Application forms for admission required information about a student's racial origin, and Akuvah discovered that the basis of admission was not academic performance, but race and gender. All applications were classified into four lists: one for Jews; another for women; the third for Slavs, Mennonites and students of other origin; and the fourth list, for Anglo-Saxon, French-Canadian and Icelandic students, was the "preferred" list. Students on the "non-preferred" list, even if they had higher averages than those on the "preferred" list, were refused admittance.

In 1944, Jewish lawyer Hyman Sokolov exposed the injustice of the "preferred list," presenting the findings of the Avukah Society to a committee of the Manitoba Legislature, with Dean Mathers and the president of the university present. After initial resistance from the university's board of governors, an investigation was launched. The accusations were verified and the university was forced to change its policy and accept students based only on academic performance, without regard to their racial origin or religion. The Manitoba medical school went on to become a progressive and successful institution despite Dr. Mathers's dire predictions at the hearing that "certain nationalities and groups" would never be accepted as doctors, and that the university would become "too Jewish."

~

During my time at the medical school, I did not experience antisemitic attitudes among students or staff except for one minor incident. During that first year, I studied hard, did well, and was awarded a medal for the highest standing in anatomy. One of the technicians working in the department said to me that he was glad that I was first and *not one of those Jews*! At the end of the year, I received one of two Isbister Scholarships, which were awarded for the highest two places at the end of our first year. I tied with Manny Shore, who was also "one of those Jews."

During the second year of studies, we took physiology, pharmacology, pathology and bacteriology. In physiology, we became the subjects in some of our class experiments. One colleague fainted when given an intramuscular injection of a hypertonic solution to experience the feeling of "visceral pain" — he obviously did! Another went into insulin shock, not uncommon in patients with diabetes, when injected with insulin.

At the end of the second year, I received a medal for the highest standing in bacteriology. As we studied various pathological disease states and saw gross specimens of diseased organs from the faculty's collection of pathological exhibits, several of us began to experience symptoms of the illnesses that we studied!

Dr. Joseph Doupe, who headed the Department of Physiology

and also lectured, was to figure prominently in my professional life. At his suggestion, I did a project on the sympathetic nerves in diabetes, working under his direct supervision, as he had done his own research in England during the war concerning the changes in the circulation in limbs affected by peripheral nerve injuries.

I embarked on my project with enthusiasm. My studies consisted of measuring skin temperature changes in response to body heating and cooling, a function governed by the sympathetic nerves, and some studies of changes in blood flow. The patients for the study were recruited at the Winnipeg General Hospital with the help of the then chief resident, Dr. John Maclean. Dr. Maclean was a wonderful human being and an excellent physician. He became my close and cherished colleague some years later.

My research with Dr. Doupe showed that indeed diabetic patients often had impaired function of the sympathetic nerves leading to the blood vessels of the lower extremities. My experience working with Dr. Doupe was invaluable. All of us who studied with him honed our skills in critical thinking during weekly seminars. We took turns presenting articles from scientific medical journals, and after the presentations, we would criticize them. Dr. Doupe would ask further critical questions that brought the methods or conclusions of the paper into question and, in essence, tore the work apart. The sessions with Dr. Doupe could be uncomfortable, but most students realized that the remarks were not personal but were intended to teach us how to assess data critically. We appreciated his interest in our development. Indeed, many of his students went on to have illustrious careers and made important contributions to their chosen disciplines.

Dr. Doupe also brought several promising researchers to the department to teach and do research. He arranged hospital positions for them as well, where they developed diagnostic, treatment and research programs that started Winnipeg on the road to excellence in medical research and health care.

While studying, I also participated in various extracurricular activities — soccer, Ping-Pong, bowling, bridge — and my dormant love of music again came to the fore. I organized lunch sessions during which I played classical records in the physiology lecture theatre. Dr. Doupe grudgingly allowed them, and they were well attended. Though Dr. Doupe did not seem to be a fan of music, others organized a "Joe Doupe" string quartet that played some concerts with a movement from Schubert's "Trout Quintet," with an added pianist, as their signature music.

During the third and fourth years, we started seeing patients in hospital clinics, usually in groups of about eight students assigned to a clinic led by a faculty member of a clinical department such as medicine, surgery and obstetrics.

In my travels to a number of Winnipeg hospitals, I became well acquainted with the local winter climate. One day, while I was waiting for a bus at the notorious intersection of Portage Avenue and Main Street, my earlobes became solidly frozen in a matter of minutes; they were as hard as blocks of wood! Luckily, there was no permanent damage.

We had a break of a few weeks after the third year. I decided to spend it in the sanatorium for patients with tuberculosis in the village of Ninette in western Manitoba. I interviewed and examined patients, and in my free time I worked on the data from the studies I had conducted with Dr. Doupe and prepared my dissertation for the degree of B. Sc. (Med.), which I would be granted when I graduated.

~

In the summer of 1953, I started my internship. At this time, most of the class lived in the old interns' residence near the Winnipeg General Hospital, which is now a part of the Health Sciences Centre complex. We were assigned two to a room in the residence and received room and board, but I don't think we were paid for our year of work and education. We worked at the General Hospital, doing monthly rotations in various specialties such as internal medicine, general surgery, urology and neurosurgery. Every few nights we were on call in the emergency department. It was in the emergency room that I performed my first surgical procedures, such as sewing up cuts and lacerations. The emergency shifts, especially at the beginning of the internship year, were very trying for me and my colleagues, as we were inexperienced. And if the night shift was a busy one, we had to do the next day's work on little sleep.

In our daily work we took histories and examined patients, following their progress under the supervision of the more experienced resident doctors and of the attending medical staff, who were in charge of the patients overall. We found that it was often helpful to obtain a patient's chart from a previous admission, and we would get the charts from the hospital records office and pore over them. There were many challenges, but we gained valuable experience. We saw and cared for a number of patients, some whom I still remember more than fifty years later.

On our time off, we held parties, some quite wild. We made day excursions to a beach on Lake Manitoba near St. Laurent in the Interlake region, one of many beaches in the province. I went out on some dates but did not form any close relationships. I was shy, and I was concentrating on my studies. We followed sporting events, especially the exploits of the Winnipeg Blue Bombers. I attended games with Ben Kitzes. My classmate Jim MacPherson played for the Bombers while in medical school as did Tom Casey, who entered the medical faculty a couple of years later.

In 1953, during our internship year, there was an epidemic of polio in Manitoba. The stricken patients were admitted to the municipal hospitals. Many not only had paralysis that affected their limbs but also had to be on respirators because of the paralysis of the respiratory muscles. Dr. John (Jack) Hildes, an associate of Dr. Doupe, was in charge and directed the operations tirelessly, going with little or no sleep for weeks on end. Respirators were flown to Winnipeg, and my classmates and I were recruited to help. I spent many shifts among the rows of respirators, tending to the sick. It was difficult to see these unfortunate victims. Dr. Hildes's efforts were recognized when the *Winnipeg Tribune* named him "Man of the Year" for battling the polio epidemic.

At the end of the year, we had to pass oral and written examinations before graduating. Although my colleagues and I passed them without difficulties, I did not get very high marks. I was surprised to be awarded a Dr. Charlotte W. Ross gold medal and prize for the highest standing in obstetrics.

After graduation, some of my classmates went into general practice. Others, including myself, continued our education with little or no break. I went on to do a year of study in internal medicine at the Winnipeg General Hospital, where I broadened my clinical experience and honed my clinical skills. During that year, I stayed in an apartment across the street from the medical school and was paid a "princely" sum of $50 a month. As part of my studies, I reviewed the current state of research on atherosclerosis (hardening of the arteries), which I presented to my colleagues. My review was published in a local medical journal of the university. I also helped a noted Winnipeg cardiologist, Dr. Robert Beamish, analyze the effects of a new anticoagulant drug. The results were published in the *Canadian Medical Association Journal*.

The following year, I completed a research study that led to my master of science degree. Dr. Doupe arranged for me to work with Dr. Mark Nickerson, who had moved from the United States to become the chair of the Department of Pharmacology. Dr. Nickerson was a world authority on the sympathetic nervous system and a contributor to a classic text of pharmacology. When I finished my work with Dr. Nickerson and completed my thesis in 1956, I was awarded a Prowse silver medal and prize.

New States and Studies

In 1954, I became a Canadian citizen. This allowed me to visit my uncle, aunt and cousin in New York. I boarded an airplane for the first time in my life, and before long saw my family after seven years apart. I looked in wonder at the mass of skyscrapers in New York and at the various sites of that unique city. My aunt and uncle lived in an apartment on the Upper West Side of Manhattan. My uncle was busy practicing ophthalmology, and my cousin Zdzich, now known as Dr. George Carter, was pursuing a specialization in ophthalmology. George's work connections helped me in planning my postgraduate studies with Dr. Irving Wright, who was an acknowledged expert in anticoagulant (blood thinning) drug studies and in peripheral vascular disease. Dr. Wright agreed that I could do a year of graduate studies in his department at the New York Hospital (now the Weill Cornell Medical Center). And so, when I finished my work with Dr. Nickerson, I set out for New York, travelling with my classmate Gerry Winkler in his Studebaker. It was an enjoyable trip, and we spent a day or two at the Atlantic Coast in Ogunquit, Maine, listening to the sound of the surf.

I found a room in the student residence associated with the New York Hospital and lived there through most of my year in New York. At the New York Hospital, I saw patients with blood vessel diseases, and at the Bellevue Hospital, I regulated anticoagulant drug treatment of patients. I became quite attached to some of these patients. I was also involved in the analysis of the results of anticoagulant treatment, which resulted in a couple of publications in prestigious medical journals.

One day, as suggested by Dr. Doupe, I went to visit Dr. Otto Loewi, a Nobel laureate in medicine in 1936, who was originally from Germany. Two years after jointly receiving the Nobel Prize, he was forced to flee the Nazis, and he eventually settled in the United States. By the time of my visit, he was quite elderly and not well, but he received me kindly.

The atmosphere of New York was exciting with its crowds and bustle. For the first time since my happy days on the sandy beaches of the Baltic Sea, I tasted delicious Italian lemon ices. I often visited my aunt, uncle and cousin. I became reacquainted with Juliette, daughter of the Kitzes family, and her husband, Marcel, and their two children. I made friends with her extended family, including Ethel, a journalist, and her brother Ben, an engineer. They were brilliant people with wide interests, and I enjoyed spending time with them.

I took advantage of New York's amazing choice of cultural events. Ben once took me to a baseball game at the Polo Grounds where the New York Giants played, and I saw the greats, Willie Mays and Bobby Thomson. I went to concerts and plays — Eugene O'Neill's *The Iceman Cometh* and *Long Day's Journey into Night*. I watched the operetta *Candide* with music by Leonard Bernstein, and I enjoyed open-air summer concerts at the Lewisohn Stadium. I even managed to see *My Fair Lady*, one of the most successful musicals on Broadway; it was still going strong in New York, and it was very difficult to obtain tickets. I was enchanted by the show. I also wanted to see a live ballet performance, which I had not done before. I finally bought a ticket to the New York City Ballet as the season was coming to a close, and I was so mesmerized by the performance that I quickly bought a ticket to another one of the remaining shows. In the spring I went on a short vacation with my former classmate Gerry Winkler, who was doing his graduate work in Boston. We went to Washington, D.C., visited the monuments and saw that wonderful city blooming with cherry trees.

During my year in New York, I went on several dates. My dates were interesting, but I was somewhat awkward, and no close relationship developed. Perhaps my teenage years that were lost during the war and the years spent in Winnipeg mostly studying left me at a disadvantage in dealing with relationships with the opposite sex. In February, I went on a date arranged through Ethel, who knew the family of my date. Her name was Emilee Horn. I went to pick her up at an apartment in the Bronx where she lived with her parents. We had dinner at a restaurant in Manhattan and went to see the musical *Li'l Abner* on Broadway. Afterwards, we had a snack and a fascinating conversation. I learned that Emilee was teaching in a city high school and had many interests, including Norse mythology, which I knew nothing about. I was impressed by Emilee and somewhat overwhelmed. While nothing between us developed at the time, more was to unfold in the future.

In 1957, Dr. Doupe arranged for me to obtain a fellowship from the National Research Council of Canada to spend a year at the Mayo Clinic in Rochester, Minnesota, in the laboratory of Dr. Wood, where I would learn new techniques of heart catheterization, useful in the diagnoses of various heart abnormalities. I eagerly took up the offer — although I knew that I wanted to return to Winnipeg to work, I was extremely interested in furthering my studies.

In late June 1957, I arrived in Rochester in a second-hand Chevrolet that I had bought from a graduate student in New York. Dr. Wood's laboratory was in the medical sciences building, which contained a human centrifuge. There, Dr. Wood and his staff studied the effects of the high gravitational forces to which pilots had been subjected during the war. After the war, the laboratory was active in pioneering various techniques to study the function of the heart and circulation in control groups and in patients with heart disease. These studies helped Dr. Wood and his colleagues diagnose patients with heart problems and give them optimal treatment.

Graduate students like me participated in the diagnostic procedures and would present the results to a panel of distinguished specialists. All students were involved in various research projects, and student researchers would recruit their fellow students for experiments. I once reluctantly agreed to be a subject for a project that involved several tubes being placed in my arteries and heart. I was apprehensive, but there were no ill effects. Being a subject for the experiment was a valuable experience because it made me realize how patients feel in similar situations and how a kind word or question that acknowledges that one is there can make a big difference in how a patient feels.

In retrospect, these experiments also demonstrated the state of research on humans, healthy and ill, in which the subjects were induced to take part in experiments that had some danger or possibility of untoward effects. Such attitudes to research prevailed for decades after World War II despite the Nuremberg Code regarding ethical research principles that was formulated at the Doctors' Trial in 1946, part of the series of Nuremberg war crimes trials. Western clinical researchers seemed to have assumed that the code was needed for the barbaric perpetrators of the atrocities of the German Reich, but not for the reasonable investigators under "normal" conditions. It was not until the 1970s that thorough guidelines and ethics committees were put in place in the medical centres of most of the western countries to protect the subjects and patients and to insist on the subject's informed consent before proceeding with the research.

The work at the Mayo Clinic was very interesting, and I met many bright physicians, students and staff members. Almost every day, I would go out for dinner with my colleagues to a local Chinese restaurant before returning to the laboratory for a few evening hours of further work or study. The projects that I was involved with led to some interesting findings that resulted in publications during the next couple of years. I heard from Dr. Doupe during this time, and we agreed that after my year at the Mayo Clinic, I would to return to Winnipeg to the Department of Physiology and set up new cardio-vascular diagnostic facilities at St. Boniface Hospital.

I often visited my classmate from Winnipeg, Sheldon Sheps, and his wife, Pearl, who were also in Rochester, as well as Dr. Gerry Vogel, a fellow in psychiatry, and his wife, Evelyn. Emilee, my date in New York, had told me about them, and I found them very interesting. They led a discussion group called Great Books, a program conceived at the University of Chicago, from where the Vogels and Emilee grad-uated. I found the book discussions in Rochester very stimulating and became acquainted with some classics of world literature.

In the fall, the Vogels told me that Emilee was coming for the Thanksgiving weekend and invited me to dinner. It was good to see her again, and we went out on a date. I was very impressed with her, intrigued by her breadth of knowledge. Emilee and I started corre-sponding regularly, and I soon realized that I wanted to marry her. I decided to go to New York for a visit in January. I asked her out and proposed. My proposal was a lengthy one, as I felt that she ought to know about Winnipeg, including its climate. Emilee accepted my proposal. I decided I would introduce her first to my cousin George. While we were in his apartment I suddenly said, "By the way, George, Emilee and I want to get married." Taken by surprise, he said, "Do you have to?" I answered, "No. We just want to!"

Emilee wanted me to know more about her roots, so we drove north of the city to an area near Peekskill, where she showed me an old farmhouse that belonged to her parents and where she had spent time in her youth. Emilee told me about her family and friends. Her mother was Jewish, and her father was Protestant and from Toronto.

Emilee was an artist. She drew, painted and sculpted. She spent time in the studio of the well-known sculptor Freeman Schoolcraft in Chicago and attended the Art Students League of New York. She took graduate courses in New York, worked at various jobs, including as a commercial artist, and obtained her teaching certificate.

My uncle Edmund met Emilee when we stopped by his office, but when I told my aunt Pola (who now often went by Pauline) that I was going to marry Emilee, she refused to meet her because she was only half-Jewish. My aunt was dead set against mixed marriages and disapproved of the non-Jewish girlfriends that my cousin George dated. Emilee once told me that a date had said to her, "Emilee, I like you, but I cannot see you anymore because you are Jewish." The very next evening she was told by another date, "Emilee, I like you, but I cannot see you anymore because you are not Jewish!" I wonder how many other children of mixed marriages are affected by such experiences.

Emilee's family threw us an engagement party at their farmhouse in the spring. Celebrations went on well into the night. I was not in a financial position to buy an engagement ring. Instead, I bought Emilee a record of Gregorian chants that she liked.

After the party, I returned to Rochester and Emilee continued her teaching. We were married in Rochester on May 31, 1958, by a justice of the peace. We had decided on a small ceremony without any family members. Emilee felt that if my aunt would not attend then her family should not be present either. We spent a brief honeymoon in a lake resort in the Brainerd region of Minnesota. Then it was once again back to finish our work in New York and Rochester respectively.

I kept busy completing my research projects at the Mayo Clinic. Emilee eventually joined me in Rochester, and we lived for the remainder of the academic year in my single-room apartment. Emilee kept it neat and helped me by typing the manuscripts of my research projects that were later published.

I got to know more about Emilee as time passed. She was only five feet tall, but no slouch at sports. She was a good baseball player and played basketball at the University of Chicago. Once, a tall opponent pushed her hard and knocked her down during a game. The big girl paid for it by later receiving Emilee's sharp elbow in her chest.

Most impressive was Emilee's teaching experience with at-risk youth at Long Island City High School in Queens, New York. She was interested in her students and helped those who needed it. She was loved by her students, appreciated by her supervisors and respected by her colleagues.

When my year at the Mayo Clinic was over, we set out on the long drive to Winnipeg where my job was soon to begin. We entered Canada at Fort Frances so that I could show Emilee the forests and lakes of western Ontario before entering the flat prairie of Manitoba.

We arrived in Winnipeg in August and stayed with the Kitzes family for a few weeks before we found a place to live, an apartment on River Avenue near the Assiniboine River. It was located conveniently close to St. Boniface General Hospital, where I was spending most of my working time. I was a member of the Clinical Investigation Unit that Dr. Doupe organized, which was headed by Dr. John Maclean. My task was to set up a laboratory to study patients with diseases of peripheral blood vessels and to introduce techniques that I had learned at the Mayo Clinic for the study of patients with heart disease.

I started doing heart catheterizations, working with one of the cardiologists at the hospital and with the surgeon Dr. Morley Cohen. In 1959, Dr. Cohen performed the first open-heart surgery in the province at St. Boniface, and I was privileged to assist. Dr. Cohen was a highly skilled surgeon, a principled teacher, problem solver and community-minded citizen who inspired others by example to better themselves and their communities.

In my clinic, I was regulating the dose of blood-thinning medications in patients who were taking such drugs on a long-term basis. I found that some other drugs that my patients were on increased the anticoagulant effect, which could potentially cause bleeding. As a result of my findings, one of these drugs was taken off the market. I supervised the anticoagulant therapy for numerous patients in the clinic at St. Boniface Hospital for more than thirty years.

I was in a good situation in the outpatient clinic because I was able to spend up to an hour taking the history of a patient and doing an examination. I would take the time to make sure that patients understood my opinion about their condition, what tests I would like to arrange and why, what the significance and prognosis of their condition was, and what options were available for treatment. I felt that spending time talking with the patients and giving them as much information as possible about their situation was important. I found that patients appreciated the time I took to examine them and talk with them when many of my colleagues did not have as much time to spend with them because of their workload and the pressure of waiting rooms full of patients.

Throughout my long career at St. Boniface, I found the people there to be helpful, caring and effective coworkers. Dr. John Maclean always remained a true and wise colleague. I think that he was one of the most underestimated members of the staff. He was an expert in endocrinology, a good teacher and a compassionate physician who cared deeply for his patients. He also established the Department of Nuclear Medicine. Foremost, however, he was a trusted friend to whom I turned many times for advice and help when I encountered problems, either work-related or personal. It was very sad when he died suddenly in 1991 on the verge of retirement. Many of us felt his loss profoundly.

With the recruitment of more cardiologists, I was able to concentrate on the investigation of peripheral vascular disease, specifically focusing on the hardening of the arteries that could lead to serious complications such as heart attacks and strokes. My work turned out to be very interesting, with different components. I also studied patients who experienced leg pain because of plugged arteries and worked with them to improve their walking, avoiding the need for surgery. My research turned to finding new ways to measure blood pressure in the legs using an ultrasonic probe, which became routine for the diagnosis and assessment of the disease of arteries in the legs.

In patients with complex presentations, the leg pressure measurement could be wrong, so I developed a way of measuring pressure in the toes and demonstrated that it was a reliable method to diagnose the presence of plugged arteries to the legs.

A doctor might be thought of as a professional who primarily takes care of patients. But since ancient times, physicians have engaged in studies or experiments to bring about new, hopefully better, ways of diagnosing and treating patients; physicians have also taught the next generation of doctors. Research and teaching have always been essential, in addition to taking care of patients. My work would come to encompass all three of these activities, which I was to find stimulating and rewarding.

Rediscovering Winnipeg

Emilee and I started enjoying life in Winnipeg — going for walks along the Assiniboine River, attending performances and entertaining friends at our apartment. Emilee became involved with the newly formed Manitoba Theatre Centre, working backstage with the props and writing articles for the theatre newsletter. The theatre, which my old friend John Hirsch directed, soon became professional and an ongoing part of the Manitoba arts scene. At the same time, Emilee enrolled at the University of Manitoba and joined a group associated with the Winnipeg Art Gallery. She would take copies of paintings to Winnipeg schools to expose students to the visual arts and enhance their appreciation of its beauty.

In 1960, Emilee became pregnant, and we started hunting for a house. In the fall, we moved to our new home on Elm Street in River Heights, a delightful neighbourhood with tall trees. Our son Joel Wacław, the middle name after my father, was born in January 1961.

When Joel turned one, we received a letter from my aunt Pauline in New York. My aunt continued to feel the loss of her son Tadzik and grieved him throughout the years, as had my uncle. In her letter of January 12, 1962, she wrote:

My dear ones,
For the birthday of the sweet child, I send you my heartfelt wishes.
That he be healthy, that he grows to give joy to the family, benefit to

people, and distinction among his co-devotees. It is a pity that I cannot be with you that day. I think about the child very often and miss him. I see in him Tadzik and ask the Highest that he possesses his strength, honest character, noble and sensitive heart, sincerity, courage, intelligence, deep faith, honourable personality and that exceptional charm that gives him the love of those who know him. I let my thoughts flow, but I do not have people to talk to about him. You know and love him, and I know that it is not a product of sick motherly imagination, but sincere truth, and that you yourself want to see in him Tadzik's qualities.

Hearty kisses,

Pola

In her later years, my aunt visited Poland, where she saw Mrs. Florentyna Krzeszewska, the mother of Danuta, who had been killed together with Tadzik; Pan Józef, the family's faithful driver from before the war; and Mrs. Zofia Rechthand from our extended family, who had helped me in the Warsaw ghetto.

When my uncle and aunt died, he in 1962 and she in 1967, I flew to New York to be with my cousin George and his family on those sad occasions.

My uncle Edmund had been a rather outgoing and cheerful person, and he appeared to adjust fairly well to his life in New York. It was therefore a surprise when, many years after his death, my cousin George showed me clippings of articles and beautiful poems in rhymed verse that my uncle contributed to *Nowy Świat* (also known as *The Polish Morning World*), a popular Polish newspaper in New York, under a pen name. The poems and articles dealt with his unabated grief over the death of Tadzik. Here is one poem that I translated:

LETTERS THAT YOU WILL NEVER RECEIVE: IN MEMORY OF MY SON

I
I write these words because I miss you
and won't believe that you're gone forever.
My hair grows grey from the sad thoughts
and a hot tear flows from my eye.

It seems to me that you're among us,
that any moment you'll open your mouth.
Devout dream deceives my senses
surrounded by silence, sad, dead and empty.

I see your face, cheerful and radiant
and hear your voice, humming a merry tune.
But in my brain pulses but one thought,
that you left and never will return.

I cannot forget your flaxen hair,
and I won't believe that you're so far.
Graveyard thoughts race through my head
And a hot tear flows from my eye.

II
I wish that you knew that here on Earth
I live and always think of you.
My feelings for you will never change
till my remains rest in a cold grave.

I wish that you knew that I'm always with you
with my being and heart and soul,
and I swear on all that is sacred
that I will never, never forget you.

I wish that you knew: love shall prevail
until the blood drains from my veins.
Ah, when you left me in this world
Happiness for me ended.

III
And yet I live, though can't understand
how one can live with my heart
ripped from my body; a precious life,
but without my soul that flew with you.

You were for me like fertile depths,
without which there can be no life here on earth.
No wonder that emptiness permeates all without you,
that despair blasphemes at times in prayer.

At times your soul deceives me in dreams.
I beg that a miracle might occur,
that you'll come to me alive, laughing,
that we'll embrace in a moment of life returned.

When my soul flew away with you,
I lost my heart, worthier than dear life.
How can the body live without one's heart?!
And yet I live, though can't understand.

IV
And when time comes for my life to end,
I wish that I dream of your face.
Easier will be to leave in my son's eyes
and lighter will be the grave above.

I wish to see you, as during the uprising.

When you promised gravely in Warsaw:
"Father! In three days, Poland will be free."
You imagined, dreamt, of true happiness.

I remember, how you stood tall
when full of hope and songs of victory.
Naive Father's heart did not think
that you shall not return.

Let sadness ebb away, dress the body,
when time comes for my life to end.
Dress in the best what remains.
I wish to sparkle when meeting my son.

v

I dreamt again that I was with you.
You were delightful and so joyful.
My heart beat happily with new vigour.
As if angels came with you.

I again dreamt that I was with you
and we talked as we did long ago.
We knew not how time was passing,
you, my happiness, my winged bird!

When you flew away from me in this world,
consciousness left my body.
I was unaware of my dreadful loss
and nothing was left of my happiness.

There came grave doctors.
They began to examine my body.
I made a better diagnosis:
My heart loved too much and broke.

~

Three years after we moved into our home on Elm Street, our second son, who we named Andrew Tadeusz to honour my cousin Tadzik, was born. Emilee was busy taking care of the family, and I carried on with my work and did some chores at home. We enjoyed gardening and went for walks around our neighbourhood. We attended social evenings hosted by my colleagues and gave a few parties at home. We would take our boys to the beautiful Assiniboine Park and its zoo and to local beaches.

For summer vacations, we would drive to Emilee's parents' farm near the Mohegan Colony in New York. It was an arduous trip with the children and took three or four days. We would also visit our families in the New York area and Emilee's friends from her youth. We spent some pleasant hours at the beach on Lake Mohegan.

As the boys grew older, we explored the beautiful sites in Alberta, including Banff and Jasper Park, and much of British Columbia as well. We also travelled through the eastern provinces and visited Toronto, Ottawa and Montreal, where we attended Expo 67.

We remained in contact with the Kitzes family and visited them regularly. They sold the store on St. Matthews Avenue and retired to a home in southern River Heights, where they enjoyed their lives for many years. Volodia succumbed to heart disease in the early 1960s, as did Mary in the 1970s.

In the mid-1970s, I was instrumental in diagnosing an aneurysm in their son, Ben, and his life was saved by emergency surgery as a result. In 1977, Val Werier, journalist for the *Winnipeg Tribune*, wrote about the event in an article titled "A Life for Old Kindnesses." Val reported on our story, how the Kitzes family had brought me, a young orphaned boy from Poland after the war, and that the boy went on to become a doctor who saved their son!

Over the years, we took advantage of the many cultural events that Winnipeg offered. At times, we were almost too busy, going out three or four times a week! We subscribed to the Manitoba Theatre Centre, the Royal Winnipeg Ballet, the Contemporary Dancers, the

Winnipeg Symphony Orchestra, the Manitoba Chamber Orchestra, and the Warehouse Theatre. Later on, the Jewish Theatre, with Beverly Aronovitch as artistic director, became an important part of our local theatre scene.

We were very happy with the quality and variety of cultural opportunities and events available in the city. We enjoyed our interest in arts — Emilee's more in visual arts and mine in music; I appreciated a chamber music series through the Virtuosi Concerts, the Agassiz Chamber Music Festival, the Winnipeg Chamber Music Society and the Musical Offering series.

My interest in playing music was revived when a colleague of mine introduced me to the recorder, the *flauto dolce* or "sweet pipe." It is an instrument very easy to start playing and enjoying, but difficult to master. Yet we were able to get together and form a group or consort that through the years varied in number from three to five players. We usually met weekly to play together as our abilities allowed. On a few occasions we played at special events at the Winnipeg Art Gallery and at the Assiniboine Park, and we participated in the annual Winnipeg Music Festival.

We introduced our sons to music: Joel took up the recorder, switched to the clarinet, and tried his hand on the saxophone and guitar, while Andrew played viola in addition to singing and acting. I had the satisfaction of playing music with my sons for pleasure and in the festival. Our younger son played with the Winnipeg Youth Orchestra and both took part in the performances of musicals put on by their schools, River Heights Junior High and Kelvin High School. Andrew was artistically inclined and attended classes at the Manitoba Theatre Workshop (now the Prairie Theatre Exchange) and performed at the Manitoba Theatre Centre and on Rainbow Stage, a delightful summer theatre in Kildonan Park.

Playing the recorder became popular and was introduced into the school curricula by the teacher Muriel Milgrom, who also played an important role in the recorder movement for adults in the province.

A chapter of the American Recorder Society was formed in Winnipeg and was active for many years, before giving way to the Early Music Society. I was a representative of the chapter, which worked well for me personally when I attended medical meetings in the United States. I would contact local members of the Recorder Society and they would invite me to play with a group, which was always a delightful evening.

Later, in Winnipeg, I bought and started learning how to play a *tenor viola da gamba*, an instrument of an old string family that was in common use before the violin family took over. Although my proficiency on the *gamba* was never as good as on the recorder, I was able to play with colleagues in a quartet or a trio of viols and found it rewarding.

~

My interest in sports began to increase when our older son, Joel, started to participate in various sports. I enrolled him in a baseball team and to my great surprise was told that I was the coach! I had never played baseball in my life. I did my best, however, and got help from an assistant coach, a father of one of the boys on the team, and very valuable help from Ben Kitzes who knew the game well and helped a lot with practices. Surprisingly, we won the local club championship in the last inning of the last game, which made everybody happy.

I was a hockey fan and followed the teams on which my son played and the Canadian National Team that was based in Winnipeg. We followed the Winnipeg Jets in the World Hockey Association and followed the 1972 Summit Series of Canada's professionals against the Soviet team and attended the game in Winnipeg. The whole family was engaged, in various ways, in sporting and cultural events.

I also sampled the game of curling, a popular Canadian winter sport, and participated in a doctor's league, which curled once a week at the Granite Club downtown near the Assiniboine River. I did some cross-country skiing too. At first, I took a few lessons with my younger son, Andrew. That was followed by more ambitious ventures that included skiing in provincial parks like Sandilands and the fable-like wonderland of the Spruce Woods Provincial Park. I also enjoyed skiing near and around the city at La Barrière Park, on the grounds of golf courses, and in Assiniboine Park, not far from where we live. I took up badminton, a game I enjoyed greatly. Although I will never master it, it is a good exercise that must have a salutary influence on my health, and I met many congenial young and older players.

At one point, my older son, Joel, who had always been a good athlete, bought me a pair of running shoes and said, "Dad, here is a pair for you. Have some fun and leave my running alone!" It was good advice; I might have been too involved. It started my jogging career, which continued throughout the early to mid-2000s, though I ran less and less as I got older. Running contributed to my well-being and relatively good health, in addition to providing many positive experiences. I took my running shoes with me on my travels to medical meetings and to vacations and they served me well over roads and pavements in many cities in North America and in England, Hawaii, Greece and France.

In Winnipeg, I participated in many road races and ran two half-marathons. I thought at first that a full marathon was too strenuous an effort, as many runners find out. In 1989, after I ran my second half-marathon at the age of sixty-one in less than two hours and felt well, I thought that I just might be able to do one full marathon. (But I kept recalling the legend of the Greek runner that ran from the village of Marathon to Athens to let the Greeks know of their army's victory over the Persians and died after delivering the news!)

In 1990, I trained more over the winter and spring leading to the annual Manitoba Marathon, an important community event that raises funds for people with intellectual disabilities. The marathon proved to be an exhilarating experience. As I jogged along Lyndale Drive, I heard a voice on a portable radio say, "An elderly male, number 307." *That's me!* I said to myself happily.

I ran by a series of humorous signs: "It is all downhill from here," "Steroids for sale" and others. At the eight-mile aid station at Harrow Street and Wellington Crescent I saw Emilee with our dog, who had come to cheer me on despite the early hour. I hugged my wife and pet the dog before resuming my trot and heard a man calling, "There is a winner!" My son Joel appeared on a bicycle around mile sixteen, keeping an eye on me, encouraging me, telling me to walk through the aid stations and take in plenty of water. I finished slowly and deliberately. It felt satisfying to enter the stadium, and the sore legs and bruises under my toenails were a small price to pay.

~

I have been very fortunate that I was able to lead a full life in which I met many interesting people and witnessed important events and natural beauty. The greater part of my life was spent in Canada, a country that has given countless immigrants like me an opportunity to live a meaningful and productive life. I was able to start a family and make a modest contribution by my endeavours. I know that I lived through my son, both of my sons, really, compensating for what I missed as a youth because of the war. I also know very well that I made things difficult for them. My wife and sons did not have it easy living with me. I was inexperienced in many aspects of life, which I attribute to my experiences during the war. Despite some ups and downs, we managed and have grown as individuals and as a family. I have learned a lot from Emilee, who knew much better than I did how to handle various situations. She was able to express her emotions spontaneously and sincerely as situations demanded. On the other hand, my emotions were held deeply in check, perhaps since the trying times in Europe when I was a teenager.

I also learned a lot from both our sons as they kept growing in age and as people. Our older son, Joel, obtained his bachelor's degree in Calgary and then worked in the cardiovascular section at the Children's Hospital of Winnipeg, took some additional courses and enrolled in medicine. He worked as an emergency room physician before taking a fellowship in palliative care, the field he continued working at in Minneapolis. In addition to his professional work, he engaged in creative writing, published a number of articles and a couple of books, and is interested in storytelling as a way of healing. He told me that he noticed that after patients in palliative care told an important story of their life, they felt generally better and their pain diminished. Joel married a wonderful young woman, Natalia, from Uruguay. We became proud grandparents of a beautiful grandson and granddaughter.

Our younger son, Andrew, followed an artistic career that took him to New York. He obtained his bachelor's and master's degrees in fine art and has worked as a dancer, choreographer and theatre director. Some years ago, we were proud to attend the performance of his successful play at the Fringe Festival in Toronto. He is also an excellent practitioner of Pilates and Feldenkrais techniques that assist people in improving and maintaining their health.

About twelve years ago, Emilee suggested that we go to a yoga class. We took classes for a couple of years, and I started to practice yoga daily. The book *Full Catastrophe Living*, by Dr. Jon Kabat-Zinn, became my guiding text. It deepened my appreciation of meditation and yoga and led to the evolution of my daily practice. It is an important part of my life that helps me maintain equilibrium, enjoy life and deal with its bumps.

Meaningful Work and Travels

As soon as I had begun working in Winnipeg, Dr. Doupe assigned a couple of my colleagues and me to teach physiology to the dental students. I was asked to teach the function of the heart and circulation, in which I was well versed, but also to teach about the kidneys and respiration. Teaching required considerable preparation as I acquainted myself with these areas of medicine. After I would come home from work and have dinner, I would spend most of the evenings studying and preparing for my lectures. I was also asked to teach medical students and have them work in the laboratory or participate in a research project. Such time commitments, which continued through most of my professional career, must have made life difficult on my family, and I was grateful for their support.

My early experiences with teaching were a learning process. I think that, at first, I was imparting to the students a large amount of information at a pace that they must have found difficult to follow and absorb. Over the years, I honed my approach to help students absorb the extensive amount of information — by printing outline notes, then creating demonstrative models of blood circulation, then an instructional video.

Over the years, I participated in courses to improve my teaching skills, and later led that course for other professors. As the medical school curriculum was being overhauled, I chaired the cardiovascular subject committee and organized a Curriculum Evaluation Seminar (CES) to obtain student feedback for the teaching faculty, which helped bring about improvements to the curriculum, and which was appreciated by the students. I was encouraged to write up the experience with CES, and my report was published in the journal *Medical Education*.

I was now guiding and supervising students, as Dr. Doupe had done for me. Sadly, Dr. Doupe had died of complications from diabetes in 1966. I was shocked and saddened when I realized during one of our meetings that he was suffering from blindness, a complication from the diabetes. I had been showing him some graphs of my data, and he looked at them and said, "It is no use." I recovered from my shock quickly and said, "Okay, I will describe them." At Dr. Doupe's funeral, I served as one of the pallbearers.

I also saw publishing articles, presenting the results of my research at conferences and publishing book chapters and reviews as having a teaching function, as my efforts contributed to the spread of new knowledge. My research was carried out with the assistance of nurses and technologists who worked with me in the Vascular Laboratory at St. Boniface Hospital and was supported by a grant from the new Manitoba Heart and Stroke Foundation; I remained a recipient of the foundation's grants for three decades.

I attended many conferences around the world, and a few of those trips were especially memorable for me, as I was able to reconnect with family and old friends. In 1970, I travelled to Europe for the first time since I had left it for Canada in 1948. The flight arrived in London, where I was reunited with my cousin Ryś. I met his wife, Doris, and daughter, Sandra. They took me to their home and were most hospitable. Ryś, who was eight years my senior, still considered me his little cousin, as was the case before the war.

My work conferences allowed me to travel to many beautiful places, but one of the most meaningful experiences for me occurred in Paris when I came across a building where my favourite Polish poet,

Adam Mickiewicz, had lived. I walked up the stairs to his apartment with awe.

During my Paris trip, I was able to see Mrs. Zofia Rechthand, who was visiting her friends in Paris from Poland. This woman was the only surviving member of the family that had helped my family and me in the Warsaw ghetto. Without their help, I would not have survived. We met for the first time since those terrifying days in September 1942. We were glad to see each other and together we reminisced. She lived out the rest of her life, mourning her husband and daughters whom she had lost in the Holocaust, in a home for the aged in Warsaw.

Over the following years, I participated in meetings in San Diego and in a number of international meetings and world congresses of cardiology in the United States, Belgium, Scandinavia, France, England, Greece and Switzerland. I was asked to contribute chapters and reviews to several publications. On a trip to Los Angeles with Emilee, we visited Stefan Halpern and his wife. He was my classmate in the secret school in the Warsaw ghetto and had become a psychologist.

In 1980, while in New York, I saw Hanna (Hanka) Herfurt, the brave gentile who played an essential role in the survival of my family, for the first time since after the war. She had finished her studies in medicine and specialized in hematology, having done postgraduate training in Boston. She married a hematologist, Dr. Gerwel, and lived in the city of Poznań, in Poland. That time in New York I remember us three — my cousin George, Hanka and me — walking down a broad avenue hand in hand.

In 1985, I flew to Israel to see the Maccabiah Games in which my son Joel was participating, running in the 800- and 1,500-metre races. I visited Tel Aviv, explored Jerusalem and its many famous sites, including the sacred sites of the three great religions. A colleague took me on a tour of the ramparts of the Old City, and I saw excavations of an ancient Roman street. I visited Yad Vashem, the museum that commemorates the Holocaust, an experience that was very moving. I saw the eternal flame burning in the Hall of Remembrance, commemorating the victims, and I walked along the avenue of the Righteous Among the Nations, where trees with plaques commemorate the gentile rescuers of the Jews. There was also a monument to Janusz Korczak, who perished in Treblinka with the children of his orphanage from the Warsaw ghetto. I went to the archives where one of the staff helped me find a document pertaining to my friend Staś with whom I had played in the early months of the German occupation in Warsaw. As Yad Vashem continued to document the lives of the victims and accept pages of testimony on family and friends who were murdered during the Holocaust, I submitted the names of my family members. Yad Vashem later grew to encompass a commemorative site and database called the Hall of Names, which contains close to three million names, and I then submitted the names of the three members of the Rechthand family and of my friend Staś Koppel.

I toured Masada and floated in the Dead Sea. I drove north to see the Sea of Galilee and visited a kibbutz close to the border with Jordan, to which my aunt Pola had made a donation to an orphanage in memory of my cousin Tadzik and uncle Edmund. I then followed a road through the mountains to the coast and north to the kibbutz founded by Holocaust survivors, including survivors of the Warsaw Ghetto Uprising. It contains the Ghetto Fighters' House Museum. There, I met a woman who knew one of my teachers in the Spójnia School in Warsaw before the war, and we spoke about the years when I was a young child in Poland, which was so meaningful to me.

∼

During the years that followed the end of the war, my memories of its horrors abated, or perhaps were suppressed. My new life had unfolded promptly in Poland, Germany and finally, in Canada, and I tried to immerse myself in it fully.

By about 1960, I was in contact with the offices of Winnipeg's Jewish community centre (known formally as the Young Men's Hebrew Association, or Y M H A) in connection with some proceedings related to reparations from Germany for Holocaust survivors, but that contact was limited. I think that I was reluctant to deal with the memories. People I came in contact with in Canada did not question me much about that part of my life. Many years later, in my extensive reading about the Holocaust and its survivors, I found that mine was not an uncommon experience, although some survivors kept reliving the horrors and suffered from nightmares. I believe that while members of the Canadian Jewish community put effort into bringing survivors to Canada and in helping them start their new lives, most were not fully aware of or interested in learning about our experiences in Europe. As time marched on, the attitudes of survivors changed.

My attitude changed around 1980. It started with a novel that a colleague recommended to me: *Mila 18* by Leon Uris, which is about the Warsaw ghetto and the uprising. At about the same time, I became aware of a symposium on the Holocaust being held at the Y M H A (now the Rady Jewish Community Centre), and I decided to attend. I soon became a member of the Holocaust Awareness Committee (H A C), which had been active for a number of years before I joined. The committee sponsored annual events associated with the anniversaries of the Kristallnacht pogrom and Yom HaShoah, commemorating the Holocaust in April and coinciding with the beginning of the Warsaw Ghetto Uprising.

Supported by the Winnipeg Jewish community, the H A C chairpersons and most of its members were, at that time, Holocaust survivors. When I joined, the chairman was Philip Weiss. I had met his wife, Gertrude, a kind and charming woman, in Munich at the Jewish Students' Union a year or two after the war. Philip had survived several Nazi camps and was passionately devoted to Holocaust remembrance. He played a vital role in the creation of the Holocaust Memorial, a monument to the victims of the Holocaust whose family members had settled in Manitoba. Built on the grounds of the provincial legislature in 1990, it was the first such monument on public grounds in Canada. On its walls are engraved the names of close to four thousand victims, including the members of my family. A solemn ceremony is held at the monument on Yom HaShoah, and government officials, leaders and members of the Jewish community, and Jewish and non-Jewish students participate.

The mandate of the HAC was to promote the memory and history of the events of that unprecedented genocide, which represented the extreme of inhumanity. I embraced that mission and continued as a committee member for many years. Like many survivors, I began to feel that our story must be told and retold.

Retracing the Past

In the summer of 1988, the Second Generation Group of Winnipeg, which consisted of children of Holocaust survivors, approached me. They were doing a project filming interviews with survivors, documenting their experiences. This was six years before Steven Spielberg's foundation (now the USC Shoah Foundation) started a large-scale project for the same purpose. I agreed to the interview, and it was recorded at the channel 9 television studios, CKND. The tapes of the interviews of the Second Generation Group of Winnipeg are a valuable resource, which was made available to the United States Holocaust Memorial Museum (USHMM) in Washington, D.C., in addition to being housed at the Jewish Heritage Centre in Winnipeg.

Later that year, after taping the interview of my experiences during the war, I was invited to an international medical meeting in Toulouse, France, to give talks related to my research interests. What was more important, however, was that I decided to go on to visit Poland. I felt that if I were ever to return to the country where I was born and grew up, now was my opportunity. I flew to Poland, and my son Andrew flew from New York to meet me the next day.

During my first evening in my hotel, I was looking through the telephone book. The book was worn out and a few years old. At the time, Poland was still ruled by a Communist government, and services and amenities were not easy to obtain. Leafing through the telephone book, I found a listing for Zdzisław Libin (now Libera), my teacher of Polish literature from the Warsaw ghetto, who I knew had survived the war. I phoned him and he remembered me well. We decided that I would contact him later during the visit and hopefully we would get together.

During the forty years that I had spent mostly in Winnipeg, I rarely spoke Polish, only when I visited my family in New York and to a few older patients of Polish or Ukrainian origin in Winnipeg, who did not speak English. But within a couple of days of my arrival, my ability to speak Polish came back and I spoke it fluently. Many people found it surprising, including my son, and at times, forgetting myself, I would start to speak Polish to him.

Andrew and I revisited the famous sites in Krakow, including the city square with St. Mary's Basilica, where the trumpeter played *hejnał* from the church tower. We toured Wawel, the grand castle of the kings of Poland with its many beautiful structures, and various historic sites, including the graves of the Polish kings and of its other famous citizens such as the poet Mickiewicz and Marshal Piłsudski. It felt good to see these sites again, which made me think back fondly to my happy childhood before the war. At the same time, it was somewhat bittersweet, as they also reminded me of when I was in Krakow soon after the war, when I first learned about the death of my dear cousin Tadzik.

I was also able to find and visit with Mr. Józef, my uncle's family's faithful driver. Mr. Józef and his wife, quite elderly by then, were glad to see us and most hospitable. It was an emotional experience for my son and me, and most likely for our hosts as well. Mr. Józef was so helpful to my family in Krakow before, during and after the war.

I contacted the local Jewish community in Krakow, and one of its members took us to the Jewish cemetery, where we went to the grave of my cousin Tadzik, after whom my son Andrew was given his middle name. Standing there again, decades after his burial, I deeply felt a sense of great loss and sadness.

We hired a driver who was also a guide and set out for Auschwitz-Birkenau and toured the infamous death camp. We were deeply affected by the sight of the crematoria and other structures and exhibits that bear witness to the atrocities that took place there during the war. On the wall in a building in Auschwitz we saw the now-famous quotation by philosopher George Santayana, "Those who cannot remember the past are condemned to repeat it."

We then went on to the resort town of Rabka-Zdrój and saw the building that housed a sanatorium, which had been co-owned by my uncle and where I spent some winter vacations as a young boy. Memories of these happy times came pouring back. We continued to Zakopane in the Tatra Mountains. I saw the familiar peak of the Giewont Mountain with its large cross, visible from the town below, which I had last seen in 1939, a few weeks before the outbreak of the war. The village seemed different than how I remembered it. It now reminded me of the crowded streets of Banff.

The next day, the driver took us on the rather long drive to Treblinka, northeast of Warsaw. The Nazis had destroyed that death camp, where my parents had likely perished. On the site are symbolic structures, stones inscribed with the names of countries Jews had been deported from; in a field were many large stones, some of them naming the cities and towns where the victims came from. One of the stones commemorates the educator Janusz Korczak. We left flowers and lit memorial candles. I was overwhelmed by a flood of emotions, thinking of my parents and hundreds of thousands of other Jews who had died a horrible death here. I think that my son was overcome by the emotions at least as much as I was.

The driver then took us to Warsaw, where we met Mr. Jan Rochwerger, who worked at the Jewish Historical Institute. Mr. Rochwerger arranged an apartment for us in the suburbs where we stayed during the rest of our visit, and he was very hospitable and helpful to us in many ways. I showed my son numerous sites that I knew from before the war. Since most of the city had been destroyed during the war, the buildings were mostly erected afterwards. I found the place where Leszno no. 22 had stood, opposite Orla Street, where I had spent my early years. Just down the street was now a small building, which, I found out a few years later, is the home of the Warsaw Chamber Opera. We walked through the Saski Garden, where I had fond memories from my childhood. Close by was the site of the Tomb of the Unknown Soldier with the honour guard and a remnant of the original building that stood there.

We went to Elektoralna Street, where my grandparents had lived before the war and where we, as well as the Rechthand family, had stayed in the ghetto. I found the site where the Spójnia School had been, and it looked similar to how I recalled it. I found Smolna Street near the large and wide thoroughfare of Nowy Świat and the building at no. 36, where we had lived for a couple of years before the war. Only the upper storeys of the building had been destroyed. Memories of these faraway times flashed before my eyes.

We visited the beautiful Łazienki Park where I had played with chestnuts before the war and where my father took me in a boat on the artificial lake around a summer palace of Poland's last king, Stanisław August Poniatowski. Near it was a stage of a summer theatre. My son struck a ballet pose for a photo. We attended a performance at the Polish National Opera.

At the Old Town Market Square, colourful buildings that I remembered from before the war had been well restored. I thought of when my father took me to the famous winery of U Fukiera when I was about seven years old and let me taste some old Polish mead. I found a place nearby where Andrew and I could drink a glass of hot mead. We saw the castle of the Polish kings and the residence of its presidents before World War II. The Germans had destroyed it during the uprising in 1944, but it was beautifully restored after the war and contains many splendid objects of art.

We next went to the Emanuel Ringelblum Jewish Historical Institute, named after the visionary historian who had established the underground Jewish archives in the Warsaw ghetto. Important documents about life in the Warsaw ghetto were hidden in sealed milk cans, two of which were recovered after the war in the ghetto's ruins. Ringelblum had lost his life there in the ruins — he was one of the many who had been found hiding on the "Aryan" side and was executed by the Germans.

The institute possessed three paintings by my aunt Stanisława Centnerszwer, which she painted in Białystok. I had, over the years, learned that my aunt and her family had gone to Białystok after the outbreak of the war, and that she and her family perished when the Białystok ghetto was liquidated in 1943. Someone named Dr. B. Czajkowska had donated the paintings after the war, but I was unable to find out who this person was. Unfortunately, we could not see the paintings because they were being exhibited in another city at the time.

My son and I next walked to the neighbourhood where, in August and September 1942, my mother and I had worked at a German factory, and then we found our way to the *Umschlagplatz*, where I had seen my mother for the last time. I was overcome with feelings of sadness and a sense of awe. My son was affected very much. There was no field there now; there was a symbolic marble gate with a rectangular enclosure as a memorial. On the inner walls were etched four hundred common first names, from A to Z, representing the hundreds of thousands of people who went through that site that led them to their deaths in the gas chambers of Treblinka.

Not far from there, we found Miła Street, the site of the bunker where the Jewish Combat (or Fighting) Organization, headed by Mordecai Anielewicz, was and where he and many fighters perished after fighting the Germans for more than three weeks in the ghetto uprising. Nearby were two significant structures: a hill with a memorial stone marking the command post and a large monument to the Warsaw ghetto fighters in the middle of a large field.

We then visited my professor from the Warsaw ghetto and his

wife; it was a bittersweet reunion as we talked about the war and about our friends and colleagues and what happened to them. I found out that my childhood friend Stefan Kraushar was now living in Urbana, Illinois, where he was a professor of sociology at the university. When I attended a medical meeting in Chicago later this same year, I contacted Stefan, and Emilee and I drove to visit with him and his family. His wife, Danuta, was a Polish gentile who had been involved in resistance work during the war. His mother, now ninety-one, lived with them and had known my mother and gone to the same school as her in Poland. She remembered me as little "Stefanek" from the pre-war years.

Another moving experience was meeting a gentile woman who was the widow of a member of the Polish underground. Her husband had participated in an abortive attempt to help the Jewish fighters in their uprising. A book she lent me describes how two Polish fighters had placed a mine in the ghetto wall in an attempt to blow a hole in it, while other members of the unit covered for them. However, a superior German force repelled the attempt and wounded some of the Polish fighters. The woman's husband, whose code name, I believe, was Kret, had participated in the skirmish.

My son and I returned to North America with many memories and photographs.

～

Twelve years elapsed before my second visit to Poland in the year 2000. At the time, my older son, Joel, who was working as an emergency room physician in Duluth, Minnesota, became very interested in seeing the places his father came from. We flew to Warsaw, from where we took a train to Krakow. Travelling by train allowed us to see the Polish countryside. Soon after we left Warsaw, the train went through the small station of Pruszków. I pointed it out to my son and told him about the events in 1944, when, among thousands of Warsaw inhabitants, I was in a makeshift camp in that town as the

Germans were winning the battle for Warsaw from the Polish underground insurgents.

In Krakow, we walked through Planty Park, the ribbon of parkland around the Old Town, and explored the numerous historic sites of that medieval city. We visited the cemetery where my cousin was buried and located the building where I had lived with my uncle and aunt shortly after the war. I again relived the moments from those faraway times and shared my memories with my son.

One evening, we had dinner at a restaurant where a young singer and two accompanying musicians provided entertainment. I asked the singer if she knew my favourite song from before the war, "Oh My Rosemary." She did and sang it beautifully. The song was appreciated by all the patrons, but especially by me, as I thought back to when I had sung it decades earlier. There was also an elderly man who was enjoying it and made a gesture of appreciation toward me.

My son and I visited the Auschwitz-Birkenau complex. In Birkenau, I closed my eyes on the platform where the selections for the gas chambers were made by the Nazis. I felt as though I were in a daze of light. My son thought that my experience might be related to the selection I had gone through at the *Umschlagplatz* in Warsaw, where I was separated from my mother in 1942. My son was deeply affected as the atrocities committed by the Nazis against the Jewish people were driven home.

We then visited Warsaw, and from there went to Treblinka, where I spent moving moments with Joel. Our hotel was in the northern part of Warsaw, not far from the site of the ghetto and the *Umschlagplatz*. We visited these sites and went to the Jewish Historical Institute. Before coming, I had been in communication with a staff member regarding my aunt's three paintings, and she had taken them out for us to see. One was a portrait of my aunt's daughter, my cousin Elżbieta. I was also given a folder full of lists of my aunt's numerous other paintings, with copies of the paintings, presumably from catalogues.

I showed my son the sites from the time when I was a youngster in Warsaw. They included the Łazienki Park, where my son struck a pose for the photo that resembled the one that my younger son had assumed there during the visit in 1988.

Somehow, I found out that the righteous woman, Hanka Herfurt-Gerwel, who lived in western Poland, happened to be in Warsaw, and we went to visit her. It was an emotional reunion, and we remained in touch afterwards. Besides Hanka, whom I knew well, I met two women about whom I had heard a lot from my cousin George. My son was very interested in meeting these women, all of whom knew my cousins and had been their good and helpful friends during the war. Hanka knew exactly where my cousin Tadzik had been killed in 1944. We went to that spot and saw a plaque that commemorated the deaths of my cousin and his friends together with many members of the Polish underground. We stood for a long time in silence near where my cousin was tragically killed.

~

On my return to Canada, I tried to find out more about my relatives and the people I knew before the war. I obtained some information through contacting USHMM and through my friend Professor Daniel Stone of the University of Winnipeg. I looked for books written by survivors from both Warsaw and Białystok, read them and contacted the authors. Irene Shapiro, who wrote *Revisiting the Shadows* was one of few survivors of the Białystok ghetto; although she did not know my aunt and uncle, she helped by expanding my list of contacts who researched the area. In *Winter in the Morning: A Young Girl's Life in the Warsaw Ghetto and Beyond 1939–1945*, the author, Janina Bauman, described several of my peers from the Warsaw ghetto. I contacted her in England; we talked about common friends and realized that we might well have known each other. Janina gave me the telephone number of one of my peers in Poland, and so it happened that in 2004, after sixty-four years, I spoke again with Hanka Kon, in whose mother's apartment we had briefly stayed in 1940 when the ghetto in Warsaw was first established.

I found it difficult to get information about my aunt Stasia and uncle Maks. I suppose that the current generation living Białystok has no connection to what happened some sixty years ago. I found some information about the musical work of Uncle Maks from before the war and about my aunt setting up an exhibit, using various items produced by the workers of the Białystok ghetto to demonstrate to the German authorities how productive and useful the ghetto's inhabitants were. One source reported that my cousin Elżbieta had married a gentile but remained with her parents and perished with them rather than trying to save herself by staying with her husband. I do not know who her husband was. I wondered whether the person who had donated my aunt's paintings, Dr. Czajkowska, might have known.

Eventually, through Yad Vashem, I found out about a man who had made a deposition about my aunt Stasia. He was living in France, and I was able to speak with him by phone. He had known my aunt, but not well. He narrowed down the date of her demise to the second liquidation of the ghetto in August 1943. I continued looking for other paintings by my aunt or a score of my uncle's musical compositions. It was a difficult task.

I was able to find out a considerable amount of information about some of my family members that has made me understand and appreciate them even more, such as names of studios where my aunt Stasia painted in Poland and in France, and articles written by my uncle Maks and honours bestowed on him. I read an opinion that his writings merited a collected edition, since they provided a prism of the musical life of Warsaw for more than two decades until World War II.

I also got in touch with a group of scholars at the Polish Center for Holocaust Research, an organization located in Warsaw that studies the Holocaust, and sent them information on my family members.[1] That information is now included online in their Warsaw Ghetto Database, which contains a lot of valuable data. I connected as well with the Warsaw Rising Museum of the 1944 Warsaw Uprising and exchanged information with their staff, including scans of photographs and documents, and with POLIN, the Polish Jewish museum in Warsaw that was collecting artifacts to display for when the museum would be built, and which opened in 2013.

Not surprisingly, the process of finding documentation on my family members has been a long one and at times frustrating. Yet, it has been most worthwhile, and on a couple of occasions I received new information when it seemed unlikely to happen. Just last year I found out that the name Dr. Czajkowska — the person who had donated my aunt's paintings — should actually be spelled Szaykowska, and that her first name was Berta. I learned that she was a known pediatrician in Białystok during the war. I also discovered that a landscape painting by my aunt that was exhibited in Warsaw in 1919 was saved and is in Warsaw. Thus, I intend to persist and continue trying to learn more.

---

1   In 2009, scholars associated with the center, Barbara Engelking and Jacek Leociak, produced the excellent book *The Warsaw Ghetto: A Guide to the Perished City* (a translation of the Polish edition, published in 2001). This book has been crucial to my own explorations, as it is extremely well researched and details life and events in the Warsaw ghetto. The authors collaborate with researchers in various countries and with Jewish scholars in Poland and elsewhere, and I've connected with Barbara Engelking many times over the years.

Returning to Music

As the years went by and I was nearing the age when many retire, I gradually started to decrease my professional commitments and began working part-time. I did less teaching and research but continued to oversee the vascular laboratory. A year into the new millennium, I gave up running the laboratory, and I retired completely a couple of years later. I was associated with the University of Manitoba for a long time — eight years as a student and forty-five as a faculty staff member. It was a most rewarding experience. I met and cooperated with numerous colleagues at the faculty of medicine, at St. Boniface Hospital and at the Fort Garry campus. Even after retiring, I audited courses at the university and used the facilities for physical activity.

The year I retired, I was pleased and surprised to be honoured with a Heart Care Award by the St. Boniface Research Centre's Institute of Cardiovascular Sciences. The gala award dinner was a wonderful evening. I was accompanied by my two sons and introduced by William Norrie, the former mayor of Winnipeg and Chancellor of the University of Manitoba. I felt humbled, particularly since Dr. Morley Cohen, the great heart surgeon who introduced open-heart surgery to Winnipeg, was given the same award at the dinner.

After my retirement, Emilee and I continued to enjoy art and events in the city at a more leisurely pace. Emilee continued to paint and garden. I listened to music and played the recorder occasionally.

I also took clarinet and was able to play some of the beloved compositions of Mozart, although not very well.

At some point, I found the copy of my friend Adam Rosenblum's
musical composition, "Symphony," which he had given me when I
was leaving for Canada. Adam was the fellow survivor I was friendly
with, the student in Munich in 1947, and I had lost contact with him
around 1951. I looked at his musical score and thought it was worth
pursuing, that I should try to do something with this piece, so I contacted composer Sid Robinovitch, who was able to convert it into a
version for piano.

On February 17, 2005, a concert took place at the Berney Theatre
at the Asper Jewish Community Campus, as part of the series *Music
'N' Mavens* under the title "Recovering Our Musical Heritage." The
program included remarks by Sid Robinovitch and some music by
him and by Ernest Bloch. I spoke about Adam Rosenblum, whom
I had known so long ago. The main highlight of the event was the
spirited rendition of Adam's work by the pianist Cheryl Pauls, which
was encored at the end of the concert. Bringing Adam's work to life
was, to me, a worthwhile endeavour, and a part of an overall effort of
many survivors to "bring back to life" the rich heritage of the Jewish
people of Europe, and in my case of Poland, where so many Jews had
once lived.

Tragically, many fine musicians were killed in the Holocaust.
What remains of their lives is their music — folk melodies, classical
and popular music, and recordings that bear witness to the Jewish
musical culture, and the Jewish and Polish music that they had created with a sense of belonging to the people among whom they had
lived for centuries. My uncle Maks was but one of these musicians. I
also well remember Alfred Schütz, the composer of "The Red Poppies
on Monte Cassino" ("Czerwone maki na Monte Cassino"), one of the
songs of World War II most cherished by the Poles.

My parents, too, had been musicians, and I kept returning to
music throughout my life. I turned to it again as my professional

activities decreased, inspired by a book I had purchased while Emilee and I were in New York visiting our families. I bought a thick volume entitled *The Mozart Compendium*, a detailed guide to Mozart — his life, his times, his personality and his music — edited by the musicologist H. C. Robbins Landon. As I read and reread the book, I also listened to CBC broadcasts that dealt with Mozart's life and covered all genres of his music. My interest in Mozart was stimulated, and I began to read a number of new biographies and listen to and collect recordings of Mozart's music.

In 2001, I decided to audit a course in the history of music of the eighteenth century at the University of Manitoba. The professor, Dr. Kurt Markstrom, was excellent and taking the course was an exhilarating experience. It was good to attend classes with a group of eager young students. I chose to participate fully, including taking tests and examinations, and completing an assignment — a detailed analysis of a musical work.

The work I chose was Mozart's "Clarinet Trio," because I heard and liked it, but also because our older son played the clarinet and the younger the viola, an unusual pairing of instruments that Mozart composed this work for with a piano. It is a unique and wonderful composition. I threw myself passionately into analyzing it, and did rather well in that assignment and in the course in general. I found the whole experience most gratifying. I also hoped that learning about the structure of compositions would allow me to understand and appreciate listening to music even more. To some extent it did in that it provided, as our professor put it, "a road map," which allowed me to follow compositions and understand what was happening as the music flowed on.

Although I had enjoyed various types of music and compositions by many classic composers, I found now that Mozart's music moved me more deeply than that of other composers. When the course ended, I felt that I somehow wanted and needed to continue. Mozart as a person, apart from his music, fascinated me. What was that man like, who gave us these invaluable gifts of his genius? I delved into Mozart family's correspondence and other sources and started writing a Mozart biography for myself.

I also found that there was a close association between music and medicine. In antiquity, music was used to treat disturbed patients; students training to become physicians were required to study music until the seventeenth century. The healing power of music has been explored to a considerable degree, and many well-known physicians have held a deep interest in music, some as musicians themselves.

I feel as though Mozart's music speaks to the soul. His works encompass the whole range of emotions: pure and simple beauty of early divertimentos and the violin concertos, exuberant joy, romance and tenderness in the *sinfonia concertante* for violin and viola and a number of the piano concertos, foreboding and dark moods in the first movements of the piano concertos K. 466 and K. 491 in minor keys, and inner emotional struggles reflected in several string quartets and quintets. Foremost is the feeling of longing in the slow movements of several piano concertos. It seems to be the longing for happiness, beauty and bliss, which humans can experience, but fleetingly.

As I made my way through studies and writing related to Mozart, a few years went by and, in 2005, I realized that 2006 was going to mark his 250th birthday. It occurred to me that there might be some interest in my work, and I found a local publishing company, Heartland Associates, to publish my book.

The year until the book launched in 2006 was memorable, culminating in the publication of *Mozart: A Meditation on His Life and Mysterious Death*. I attended concerts, signed my book and gave several talks and presentations about Mozart and his music. Talking about Mozart was, for me, delightful, and I very much enjoyed being master of ceremony at a special concert of Mozart's music at St. Bartholomew's Anglican Church in Winnipeg in October 2006.

Epilogue

Throughout the 1990s and 2000s, I was committed to Holocaust education in Winnipeg. On the occasion of the fiftieth anniversary of the Warsaw Ghetto Uprising, which was commemorated in ceremonies around the world, including in Warsaw, I was briefly interviewed by the Canadian Broadcasting Corporation (CBC), which ran a segment in the local news. That same year, I participated for the first time in a presentation on the Holocaust and other genocides at Oak Park High School. For the students, having an opportunity to hear from survivors was an extremely important part of the presentation. This educational outreach program was an initiative of retired Winnipeg teacher Hersch Zentner, a Canadian who did not experience the Holocaust, but who worked tirelessly to bring Holocaust education to schools throughout Manitoba.

As the landscape for Holocaust education in Winnipeg grew, I worked alongside Philip Weiss and Barbara Goszer as part of the Holocaust Awareness Committee, editing the biannual newsletter, *The Holocaust Remembered*. In 1997, the newly founded Asper Jewish Community Campus expanded and through the tireless work of Barbara Goszer and her colleagues, grew to house the Freeman Family Foundation Holocaust Education Centre in the Jewish Heritage Centre (JHC) of Western Canada. There, a memorial wall with plaques commemorates victims of the Holocaust and pays tribute to the righteous gentiles, acknowledging contributions made by individuals and families I sponsored a plaque that acknowledges Dr. Hanna Herfurt-Gerwel, Zofia Różycka and Danuta Krzeszewska, the three Polish women without whose help and courage my family members and I would not have survived the war.[1]

The JHC organizes a large annual Holocaust symposium for high school students, and teachers prepare their classes to listen to a keynote presentation and participate in breakout sessions in which a Holocaust survivor tells their story. Over the past two decades, I've continued to make presentations to classes of high school and university students and participate in these symposia.

Holocaust education further developed with the Asper Foundation's Human Rights and Holocaust Studies Program. The program, which has become a national initiative, generates awareness of the Holocaust by educating students in Grades 7 to 9 about racism and antisemitism, and culminates in a trip to the Canadian Museum for Human Rights in Winnipeg.

On Yom HaShoah in Winnipeg, Holocaust survivors, members of the Jewish community, and non-Jews — including public and government figures — read the names of the victims of the Holocaust and where they perished at a ceremony in the parliament building. This is connected to a program started by B'nai B'rith called Unto Every Person There Is a Name. In 2002, I read the names of my family members, further personalizing, to some extent, the anonymous millions who were killed in the Holocaust.

Thinking about the monument at the parliament building, with the nearly four thousand names read at the ceremony, made me think that it might be worthwhile to try to "bring back to life" the

---

1   In 2015, I was instrumental in having Dr. Hanna Herfurt-Gerwel, Zofia Różycka and Florentyna and Danuta Krzeszewska formally recognized by Yad Vashem as Righteous Among the Nations.

people, their lives and culture that were lost during World War II. In 1997, I proposed to the HAC a project called the Manitoba Holocaust Heritage Project, which would document the pre-war lives of the murdered Jewish individuals whose names appear on the monument. The project was approved, and survivors or their descendants were asked to fill out questionnaires and provide stories about pre-war life. Despite the hard, unselfish work of a number of devoted volunteers, however, the project continued to linger until Belle Jarniewski (then Millo), chair of the Holocaust Education Centre, took it upon herself to put together the information and stories of over fifty survivors and their families. Belle, now executive director of the JHC, spent countless hours typing and tirelessly working to obtain support for the book, *Voices of Winnipeg Holocaust Survivors,* which was published in 2010.

Holocaust survivors and their descendants have talked and written about their experiences to memorialize their murdered families and to bring about greater tolerance, and thus a better world. I believe we are achieving the first objective, but the second remains elusive as antisemitism continues unabated and other genocides are taking place. On an individual level, I have found that teaching people about the Holocaust generally evokes expected and appropriate reactions from audiences. I have received heartfelt letters from students in the schools where I made presentations, and I was thanked by many individual students and teachers after I told them about my experiences. Many felt moved, and I hoped that at least some would adopt more positive attitudes toward students with different backgrounds.

In addition to educating people about the effects of racism and antisemitism, other strategies that have been identified as important in promoting understanding and respect for people who are different from oneself include understanding one's own emotions, the ability to think critically and opportunities to meet with members of other communities. There is a need for more interaction among various ethnic groups, and in Winnipeg, I took part in an important conference called Building Bridges that brought together members from Jewish, Mennonite and Ukrainian communities, where presentations on interactions and concerns aimed to bring people closer together.[2] Personally, I would welcome a meeting of Polish and Jewish groups in Canada. I feel an affinity with and appreciate the cultural contributions of both these nationalities.

Unfortunately, I don't think that teaching people about the Holocaust has resulted in a wider, overall change in antisemitic attitudes. "Never again" emblazoned on memorial stones at the site of Nazi death camps in several languages rings hollow. In Canada, antisemitic incidents as compiled by B'nai B'rith have increased from the annual rate of seventy-seven in the early 1980s to 258 in the 1990s and to 829 by the year 2005. By 2017, and up to 2020, the annual rate had risen to more than two thousand antisemitic incidents in each of those three years.

I do still believe that Winnipeg, with the establishment of the Canadian Museum for Human Rights, and Canada in general, are now in the forefront of the promotion of the human rights, a tremendous progress compared to sixty years ago. It will always be necessary, however, to fight prejudice and to try to prevent genocides and abuses of human rights. We must continue our efforts and take measures in these endeavours. Among them we must always keep remembering the Holocaust, because it is our solemn trust to commemorate its victims, and because the Holocaust provides a focal point that lends itself well as the trigger to counteracting hate and racism. To forget it would foster indifference, which was an important factor in

---

2   The conference was organized by the Jewish Historical Society (which later amalgamated into the JHC), the Manitoba Mennonite Historical Society, and the Manitoba Eastern European Heritage Society, and its proceedings were later published. Fred Stambrook and Bert Friesen, eds., *A Sharing of Diversities: Proceedings of the Jewish Mennonite Ukrainian Conference, "Building Bridges"* (Regina: The Canadian Plains Research Center, 1999).

its perpetration. The Holocaust stirred the conscience of the people of the world by the stark demonstration of humanity's ability to inflict evil, and learning from that plays an important part in generating harmony among us all.

I think it is essential to study, together with the Holocaust, many other catastrophes, genocides and large-scale injustices, which continue to occur while the world remains largely indifferent. Extreme human suffering must be acknowledged, and there is no need for competition for martyrdom. Even though the Holocaust was unique in the extent and "scientific" methods that the highly cultured Nazis used, the deaths and suffering of many millions of the victims of other genocides are an equally essential ingredient of our collective human remembrance and important in the common fight for freedom from discrimination and injustice.

~

Over the years, I have wondered, as have other survivors of the Holocaust, why I survived, why I was among those few that denied the Nazis their desire to annihilate us all. I felt, as do others, that luck played a large part, but undoubtedly, I would not have survived without the members of my family and the righteous Polish gentiles, who were an integral part of this story. I hope that they will always be remembered. I wondered what I would have done if I were the one who saw, from the outside, what the Nazis were doing to the Jews. Would I have acted to help the victims or stood silently by, indifferent or fearful for my own safety? I do not know. Humans, when in power, have ways of manipulating others in various ways, apart from threats and torture. Yet, individuals have personal and group resources that can allow them to resist pressures and thwart the criminals.

One major predictor of gentile heroism was membership in a socially active group: religious, political or even recreational. Group membership promoted social solidarity and broke down the isolation that contributed to people conforming to Nazism. And so, one way to generate more tolerance is to promote socially conscious activities of all kinds.[3]

The close to thirty thousand gentiles recognized by Yad Vashem in Jerusalem as Righteous Among the Nations for saving Jews during the Holocaust are only a small percentage of gentiles who helped Jews. Many heroic gentiles eluded recognition because the Jews they protected died without giving testimony, because some of the gentiles preferred anonymity or because Yad Vashem's definition is restrictive. Additional thousands or even much larger numbers performed small acts of heroism and simple decency that helped Jews survive. For example, villagers who knew that their neighbours were hiding or helping Jews and chose not to turn them or the Jews in, or those who shared their own limited food supplies with Jews in hiding. Many deserving gentiles risked death at the hands of the Nazis but were denied official recognition because they took money from Jews to feed them and to bribe suspicious guards. So many Holocaust survivors owe their lives to the assistance of heroic gentiles, and to numerous gentiles who chose not to act villainously despite rewards that the Nazis offered.

There were many reasons for such heroism. Some gentiles saved friends and neighbours. Some saved strangers because they hated injustice. Some saved Jews to resist the Nazis. Some responded when a Jew came to ask for help. Some responded to an approach by a gentile friend to share the burden of saving a Jew. Some devout Christians saved Jews in accordance with Christian dogma to love their neighbours, including priests who supplied baptismal certificates. Some atheists saved Jews out of socialist idealism. Some belonged to resistance organizations.

In Poland, righteous gentiles were responsible for the survival of

---

3   My research on the righteous is largely based on an article by University of Winnipeg professor emeritus Daniel Stone titled "Gentile Heroism during Holocaust," written for the Holocaust Awareness Committee in Winnipeg.

many Jewish people, including me and members of my family. Jews who were hiding in the "Aryan" part of Warsaw were in constant danger of being blackmailed by antisemites and criminals, rendered penniless, or denounced to the German authorities. Chances of survival for Jews who tried to "pass" as gentiles were enhanced by a perfect command of the Polish language, financial means, "good looks" (as in, not stereotypically Jewish), and confident deportment, which many hunted Jews lacked.

An underground organization for the purpose of helping Jews, called Żegota, was formed in Poland in 1942. Żegota, the Council for Aid to Jews, included righteous Poles who worked with members of Jewish organizations, and was organized in part by Polish Catholic activists. Żegota helped thousands of Jews in Warsaw and other large cities by organizing hiding places outside of the ghetto, supplying false papers and food, and finding trustworthy doctors for them when they were sick. Among individuals that were part of Żegota was Irena Sendler, a health worker and remarkable woman. She saved more than 2,500 Jewish children by smuggling them out of the Warsaw ghetto to safe hiding places and found non-Jewish families to give them shelter. Although she was caught and tortured, she would not divulge any information.[4]

There were righteous gentiles in every country, including Germany, who helped Jews.[5] Those who have been named Righteous

---

4   In *Secret City: The Hidden Jews of Warsaw, 1940–1945* (2002), scholar Gunnar S. Paulsson estimated, in an extensive, well-researched study, that about 11,500, or 40 per cent, of the Jews who hid in the "Aryan" part of Warsaw survived the war.

5   One book about a remarkable rescue of German Jews is *The Greatest Invention of the Leitz Family: The Leica Freedom Train* (2002), by Frank Dabba Smith. The Leitz family, who manufactured Leica cameras before World War II, rescued hundreds of Jews by smuggling them out of Germany as their "employees" to be stationed abroad. One member of the Leitz family was imprisoned for these efforts. Until the death of the last member of the family, their wishes did not allow the publication.

Among the Nations were the shining light during the darkness of the Holocaust; possibly, their actions hold clues that might be helpful in humankind's efforts to improve society. The stories of their valour are inspiring. While large numbers of their heroic deeds will never be known, the more we know about them, the more we are likely to appreciate them and benefit from them.

It would be wonderful if we could distill the essence of gentile heroism and inject it into the world's population to protect all peoples from racism. That might entail application of empathy to our fellow human beings and accommodation of the distinctly human need for "recognition."[6] While recognition can have deleterious effects — competition for prestige, or, in its most heinous form, the biological instinct of self-preservation above all else — it is likely also the force that leads to creativity and new developments. Over the course of recent history, civilization has progressed immensely, including the development of liberal democracy ("the end of history"), a political system that provides its citizens with "recognition" based on the principles of freedom and equality. Yet, freedom and equality are mutually limiting, as my professor of history taught me in the clandestine school in the Warsaw ghetto.

In the liberal democratic countries of today, freedom allows some people to become very successful and much more recognized than others, rendering society unequal. In between, the middle class forms a large proportion of the population and contains many grades of "equality." Thus, human history does not seem to have ended. The fine-tuning of the checks and balances of liberal democracies needs to be constantly attended to in order to maintain a necessary balance between freedom and equality.

---

6 Francis Fukuyama discusses this concept in his book *The End of History and the Last Man* (2002).

Perhaps empathy is the key, equivalent to the third part of the motto of the French Revolution — Fraternité, which may be necessary to provide the balance to the Liberté and Égalité. Now it is but a hazy dream in a distant future and it might not be feasible or even desirable, if it would entail interference with the innate drive for recognition that fuels human striving and defines what it means to be human. In the future, humanity must proceed with great caution and consider how to balance and guard against unintended and deleterious consequences of recognition. The world of our children is infinitely more complex than ours was. I wish them and subsequent generations wisdom and success.

Glossary

antisemitism Prejudice, discrimination, persecution or hatred against Jewish people, institutions, culture and symbols.

Aryan A nineteenth-century anthropological term originally used to refer to the Indo-European family of languages and, by extension, the peoples who spoke them. It became a synonym for people of Nordic or Germanic descent in the theories that inspired Nazi racial ideology. "Aryan" was an official classification in Nazi racial laws to denote someone of pure Germanic blood, as opposed to "non-Aryans," such as Slavs, Jews, part-Jews, Roma, and others of supposedly inferior racial stock.

circumcision Removal of the foreskin of the penis. In Judaism, ritual circumcision is performed on the eighth day of a male infant's life in a religious ceremony known as a brit milah (Hebrew) or bris (Yiddish) to welcome him into the covenant between God and the People of Israel.

displaced persons (DP) camps Facilities set up by the Allied authorities and the United Nations Relief and Rehabilitation Administration (UNRRA) in October 1945 to resolve the refugee crisis that arose at the end of World War II. The camps provided temporary shelter and assistance to the millions of people — not only Jews — who had been displaced from their home countries as a result of the war and helped them prepare for resettlement.

displaced persons (DPs) People who find themselves homeless and stateless at the end of a war. Following World War II, millions of people, especially European Jews, found that they had no homes to return to or that it was unsafe to do so. To resolve the staggering refugee crisis that resulted, Allied authorities and the United Nations Relief and Rehabilitation Administration (UNRRA) established displaced persons (DP) camps to provide temporary shelter and assistance to refugees, and help them transition toward resettlement. *See also* United Nations Relief and Rehabilitation Administration (UNRRA).

Doctors' Trial A war crimes trial held in Nuremberg, Germany, that began on December 9, 1946, and charged twenty-three German doctors and administrators with war crimes and crimes against humanity for their roles in murdering people with disabilities and experimenting on prisoners held in Nazi camps. Of the sixteen doctors found guilty by the American-run court, seven were sentenced to death. Questions of medical ethics became central to the case, and the defence pointed out that there were no existing international laws defining legal or illegal human experimentation. An important outcome of the 1947 verdict was the creation of the Nuremberg Code, which outlined ethical protocols for experimentation on humans, including the principle of informed consent. Today, scientists reject the use of results from Nazi medical experiments, given the conditions and questionable standards under which they were conducted.

Final Solution (in German, Die Endlösung der Judenfrage) An abbreviation of the euphemistic term the "Final Solution to the Jewish Question," the Nazi plan for the systematic murder of Europe's Jewish population between 1941 and 1945.

Jewish Council (in German, Judenrat) A group of Jewish leaders appointed by the German occupiers to administer the ghettos and carry out Nazi orders. The councils tried to provide social services to the Jewish population to alleviate the harsh conditions of the ghettos and maintain a sense of community. Although the councils appeared to be self-governing entities, they were actually under complete Nazi control. The councils faced difficult and complex moral decisions under brutal conditions — they had to decide whether to cooperate with or resist Nazi demands, when refusal likely meant death, and they had to determine which actions might save some of the population and which might worsen their fates. The Jewish Councils were under extreme pressure and they remain a contentious subject.

Jewish ghetto police (in German, Ordnungsdienst; Order Service) The police force that reported to the Jewish Councils, under Nazi order. The Jewish ghetto police were armed with clubs and carried out various tasks in the ghettos, such as traffic control and guarding the ghetto gates. Eventually, some policemen also participated in rounding up Jews for forced labour and transportation to the death camps, carrying out the orders of the Nazis. There has been much debate and controversy surrounding the role of both the Jewish Councils and the Jewish police. Even though the Jewish police exercised considerable power within the ghetto, to the Nazis these policemen were still Jews and subject to the same fate as other Jews.

Kennkarte (German, pl. Kennkarten) Official civilian identity documents issued by the German authorities in occupied Europe during World War II. Kennkarten were issued to various groups and distinguished by colour: grey for Poles, yellow for Jews and Romas, and blue for Russians and other non-Polish Slavic peoples.

Narodowe Siły Zbrojne (NSZ; National Armed Forces) An underground Polish right-wing resistance organization established in 1942 to fight the German occupation, Soviet partisans and communists. The NSZ continued to carry out attacks on communist institutions after the war and on Jews who were returning to their homes in Poland after the Holocaust.

Polish Home Army (in Polish, Armia Krajowa) Also known as AK or the Home Army, the Polish Home Army was the largest armed resistance movement in German-occupied Poland during World War II. Originally formed in 1939 as the Związek Walki Zbrojnej (Union of Armed Resistance), the movement was renamed in 1942 and began to integrate other Polish underground forces under its umbrella. Although it has been criticized for antisemitism, and some factions were even guilty of killing Jews, the AK also established a Section for Jewish Affairs that collected information about what was happening to Jews in Poland, coordinated communications between Polish and Jewish resistance organizations, and supported the Council for Aid to Jews. Hundreds of Jews joined the AK, and members of the AK assisted the Jewish resistance during the Warsaw Ghetto Uprising in 1943. In August 1944, the AK started an uprising to liberate Warsaw from German occupation, but they were defeated in October 1944. *See also* Warsaw Ghetto Uprising.

Righteous Among the Nations A title given by Yad Vashem, the World Holocaust Remembrance Center in Jerusalem, to honour non-Jews who risked their lives to help save Jews during the Holocaust. A commission was established in 1963 to award the title. If a person fits certain criteria and the story is carefully checked, the honouree is awarded with a medal and certificate and is commemorated on the Wall of Honour at the Garden of the Righteous in Jerusalem.

Star of David (in Hebrew, Magen David) The six-pointed star that is the most recognizable symbol of Judaism. During World War II, Jews in Nazi-occupied areas were frequently forced to wear a badge or armband with the Star of David on it as an identifying mark of their lesser status and to single them out as targets for persecution.

Treblinka A Nazi death camp in German-occupied Poland about eighty kilometres northeast of Warsaw, established in 1942. Treblinka was the third death camp built specifically for the implementation of Operation Reinhard, the planned mass murder of the Jews in occupied Poland. The first massive deportations to Treblinka were from Warsaw and began on July 22, 1942. Inmates of the camp staged an uprising in August 1943 and hundreds of prisoners escaped, but the majority of them were caught and killed. Treblinka was dismantled in the fall of 1943. Approximately 900,000 Jews and unknown numbers of Poles, Roma and Soviet POWs were killed in Treblinka.

United Nations Relief and Rehabilitation Administration (UNRRA) An international relief agency created at a 44-nation conference in Washington, DC, on November 9, 1943, to provide economic assistance and basic necessities to war refugees. It was especially active in repatriating and assisting refugees in the formerly Nazi-occupied European nations immediately after World War II.

Warsaw ghetto A small area in the city of Warsaw where approximately 400,000 Jews were forced to live beginning in October 1940. Enclosed by a ten-foot wall, the ghetto's horrific conditions led to the death of 83,000 people from starvation and disease. Mass deportations from the ghetto to the Treblinka killing centre were carried out between July and September 1942.

Warsaw Ghetto Uprising A large rebellion by Jewish resistance fighters in the Warsaw ghetto, beginning on April 19, 1943, and lasting several weeks. After the mass deportation and murder of ghetto inhabitants in the summer of 1942, resistance groups prepared for an uprising. In January 1943, the Nazis attempted to deport the remaining Jews, but they encountered armed resistance and suspended deportations. When the Nazis entered the ghetto to deport the remaining inhabitants in April 1943, about 750 organized ghetto fighters launched an insurrection, while the other inhabitants took shelter in hiding places and underground bunkers. The resistance fighters were defeated on May 16, 1943, resulting in the destruction of the ghetto and the deportation of the remaining

Jews; more than 56,000 Jews were captured and deported, and about 7,000 were shot.

Warsaw Uprising An uprising by the non-Communist Polish resistance movement, the Polish Home Army (AK), to liberate Warsaw from German occupation and take control of the city before the Soviets arrived. The uprising started on August 1, 1944, as the Soviet army neared the city from the east. Facing a severe shortage of supplies and a calculated lack of support from the Soviets, the AK's approximately 40,000 troops were defeated by October 2, 1944. The revolt resulted in the deaths of over 150,000 civilians and the further destruction of a significant portion of the city. About 85 per cent of Warsaw had been destroyed by the time the city was taken over by the Soviets and the pro-Soviet First Polish Army in January 1945. *See also* Polish Home Army.

Photographs

1 Stefan's father, Wacław Reicher, before the war. Place and date unknown.

2 Stefan (right) skiing with his aunt Pola (Pauline) on vacation in the Tatra Mountains. Poland, 1936.

3 & 4 Stefan with his mother, Janina (right; and centre), and his aunt Pola on their last holiday before the war. Zakopane, Poland, August 1939.

1

2

3

1 The Rosenhauch family before the war. Left to right: Stefan's cousin Zdzich, his aunt Pola, his cousin Tadzik and his uncle Edmund (Mundek). Place and date unknown.

2 Stefan's cousin Tadeusz (Tadzik) Rosenhauch, in a photo taken during his time as a medical student at Jagiellonian University. Krakow, Poland, circa 1937.

3 Tadzik's girlfriend, Danuta Krzeszewska, who was killed alongside Tadzik during the Warsaw Uprising. Place and date unknown. Photo courtesy of the Righteous Among the Nations database, Yad Vashem, Jerusalem.

1

2

3

4

1 Florentyna Krzeszewska, who helped Stefan's relatives survive the Holocaust. Photo courtesy of the Righteous Among the Nations database, Yad Vashem, Jerusalem.

2 Stefan's uncle Maks Centnerszwer, in a clipping from *Nasz Przegląd* (Our Review). Warsaw, Poland, 1933.

3 Stefan's aunt Stasia Centnerszwer, featured in an issue of *Nasz Przegląd* (Our Review). Warsaw, Poland, 1930.

4 Aunt Stasia's painting of her daughter, Elżbieta. Białystok, Poland, date unknown. From the collections of the E. Ringelblum Jewish Historical Institute.

Stefan's high school certificate. Krakow, 1946.

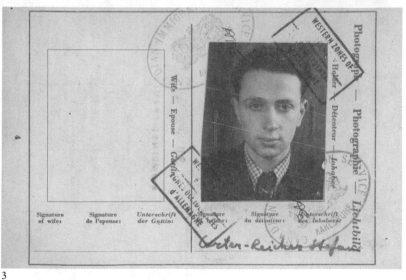

1 Stefan (right) with his cousin Zdzich (George) after the war. Munich, Germany,
   1947.
2 Stefan's cousin Ryś and his wife, Doris, who Stefan reconnected with after the
   war. Place and date unknown.
3 Stefan's immigration visa, issued in Germany in 1948.

1   Stefan after immigrating to Canada, in front of the house where he lived with the Kitzes family at 657 St. Matthews Avenue. Winnipeg, circa 1950.

2   Stefan with Volodia Kitzes. Winnipeg, circa 1950.

3   Stefan with Mary Kitzes on St. Matthews Avenue. Winnipeg, circa 1950.

4   Stefan with Etta Brenner, who asked her family to sponsor Stefan to live with them in Winnipeg. Circa 1950.

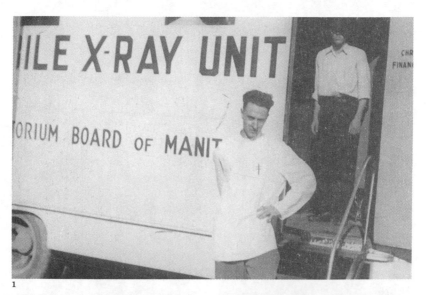

1

2

3

1 Stefan as a medical student while working for a mobile X-ray unit for a tuberculosis prevention program. Manitoba, 1950.

2 Stefan's graduation photo from the University of Manitoba, Faculty of Medicine. Winnipeg, 1954.

3 Stefan and his wife, Emilee, at the Kitzes family home after moving to Winnipeg together. September 1958.

1 Emilee and Stefan, circa 1970s.
2 Emilee and Stefan. Winnipeg, 1970.
3 Emilee and Stefan. Winnipeg, circa 1980s.

1 Stefan reuniting with Mr. Józef and his wife, name unknown. Krakow, Poland, 1988.

2 Stefan with Hanka (Hanna) Herfurt-Gerwel (centre) and her friends. Warsaw, Poland, 2000.

1 Stefan's son Andrew with Zdzisław Libera (formerly Libin) and his wife, name unknown. Stefan reconnected with Zdzisław, his teacher of Polish literature in the secret school in the Warsaw ghetto, while on his first trip back to Poland with Andrew. Warsaw, 1988.

2 Stefan in front of the building that used to be his aunt Pola and uncle Edmund's villa. Krakow, 1988.

3 Stefan with his son Joel at the Treblinka memorial site. Poland, 2000.

1 Stefan with his family. Left to right: Stefan's wife, Emilee, his son Joel, his son Andrew, Stefan, and Joel's wife, Natalia. Winnipeg, 2005.
2 Stefan with his sons, Andrew (left) and Joel (right), on the occasion of Stefan's ninetieth birthday. Winnipeg, 2018.

Appendix: Dealing With the Legacy of the Holocaust

Editor's Note: Until 2022, Stefan Carter had been working on a new book titled *Anatomy of the Holocaust and Its Aftermaths: A Window into Human Nature*. He had written approximately one hundred and fifty pages and had been hoping to have his work published. His work was divided into the following subjects: the world before World War II; the question of how the Holocaust could have happened and how it did happen; responses of the perpetrators and victims; responses in Nazi-controlled countries and in countries outside Nazi control; dealing with the history of the Holocaust; Polish-Jewish relationships; and the world after World War II. The following content offers some of his earlier explorations into these issues.[1]

Over the years, as I worked to preserve the memory of the Holocaust, I also read extensively and thought about what transpired during those terrible times. How could the German state carry out a systematic killing of six million Jews, in addition to hundreds of thousands of Roma, people with disabilities, and tens of thousands or more homosexuals, political dissidents and millions of members of other occupied nations, and how could the rest of the world allow it

---

1 All sources for this material as well as for prior chapters are in the bibliography at the end of the appendix.

to happen? This question has generated a huge volume of literature and scholarly discourse. Despite the outpouring of scholarly writings for more than fifty years, there is no simple answer to the question of how the enormous evil of the Holocaust, perpetrated by a highly cultured European nation, could have taken place. The events defy comprehension. Yet even an incomplete understanding helps us dissect the complexity of the events and can provide insight into human nature and other genocides.

In my understanding, since the dispersal of the Jewish people in the Diaspora, the majority of Jews tended to follow their religious and cultural customs wherever they settled, rather than assimilate. Although some became successful in various endeavours and contributed to the economic and cultural lives of their adopted countries, they were repeatedly used as scapegoats whenever things did not go well. Jewish communities were persecuted because they were different and because of the antisemitic attitudes of the Catholic church, which most Protestant churches followed.

In Poland, Jews faced limitations in commercial opportunities, which resulted in severe economic hardships and poverty for the masses of the Jewish people who were not assimilated. In contrast to the assimilated minority, most Jews lived relatively isolated from the country's Catholic population, used their own Yiddish language, and followed their social and religious ways. Many had a poor ability to speak the Polish language and limited exposure to Polish culture. At the same time, they often provided a useful service to the Polish population in the form of trade, making many items available in their stores that people needed.

Marshal Józef Piłsudski, who governed Poland after staging a coup in 1926 until his death in 1935, was thought to be relatively friendly toward the Jews. After his death, however, antisemitic policies of the Polish government increased virulently, despite some opposition from moderate factions mostly from the political left. The Polish government actively sought a solution to "the Jewish problem" by looking for places where Polish Jews could emigrate, for example to Palestine and the island of Madagascar, and even discussed the problem with Hitler.

Hitler's ascent to power is said to have taken place at least in part because of the economic depression, as well as the resentment of the Germans because of the conditions imposed on them after World War I. I believe, as well, that so-called scientific thought contributed to Hitler's rise and ideologies — well before the Nazi regime came to power. Darwin's theory of evolution led to the development of eugenics aimed at preventing the reproduction of humans judged to be "defective" and thus detrimental to the human species. A Racial Hygiene Society was formed in Germany as early as 1905, and utilitarian views, which held that it would be acceptable to prevent reproduction and even "exterminate" the physically or socially unfit, were adopted. Other branches and affiliated organizations were established internationally — in Sweden, the United Kingdom, the Netherlands and the United States.

Sterilization of 38,000 people, mostly racialized people with cognitive disabilities, took place in the United States between 1908 and 1941 and was deemed constitutional by the Supreme Court. This large-scale practice continued into the early 1970s — more than 60,000 people were sterilized in the United States in the twentieth century — and forced sterilizations in the United States have occurred as recently as 2010. Canada, as well, had sterilization laws in two provinces, Alberta and British Columbia, from the late 1920s and early 1930s until the early 1970s. But the biggest sterilization programs were those in Nazi Germany, which sterilized over 400,000 individuals in the 1930s and 1940s; even more horrific was the Nazi regime's T4 program, which murdered 275,000 people with disabilities. Secretly recruited members of the German medical profession took on an essential role in carrying out the large-scale annihilation, planning and supervising the killings, and taking opportunities to carry out inhumane research experiments.

In parallel to conceptualizing and abusing the rights of the "unfit," immigration laws were also at play: in 1924, the US Congress passed an Immigration Act that barred immigrants from Asia and restricted immigrants from Eastern Europe, largely for racial reasons. As persecution against German Jews rose in Nazi Germany, there was practically nowhere for them to flee, as evidenced by the summer of 1938, when delegates from thirty-two countries met at Évian-les-Bains in France to discuss the issue of hundreds of thousands of German Jews who were trying to flee the Nazi regime. Over nine days, delegates debated the fate of refugees, but most countries, including the United States and Britain, did not change their restrictive immigration policies.

The western countries — Britain, the United States and Canada — overall remained aloof toward the plight of the Jews when Hitler came to power and during the war. This was largely because of government officials' antisemitic views; people who were in positions of power did not save Jews. Canada interned Jews from Germany in prisoner-of-war camps, just as they did with German nationals and those of Japanese origin.

In addition to ingrained and worldwide antisemitism, the unprecedented inhumanity and extent of the Holocaust made it difficult for people to believe that it was really occurring. However, reports of the annihilation of the Jews that was taking place near the Eastern Front and in Poland were communicated early to the West. First, there were reports of the mass killings by the German Einsatzgruppen in the occupied Soviet territories in 1941. Then a German industrialist, Eduard Schulte, informed associates in Switzerland in 1942 about the imminent threat of Hitler's "Final Solution."

Several couriers, messengers who travelled from Poland to England, reported the mass murders to the Polish government-in-exile in London and to British and American authorities. Jan Karski, a righteous gentile and the subject of the book *Karski: How One Man*

Tried to Stop the Holocaust, was the first of the Polish couriers. He went into the Warsaw ghetto in August 1942, when a large proportion of the ghetto population was being taken to Treblinka, and then he was smuggled into the Izbica ghetto in Poland, which functioned as a transit camp. There he witnessed masses of Jews being treated inhumanely, and he saw Jews packed into train cars to be deported to their deaths. His report tended to be met either with indifference or disbelief in the grim reality.

A second Polish courier, Jan Nowak, who wrote the memoir *Courier from Warsaw*, reported that a Jewish member of the Polish government-in-exile in London, Isaac Schwarzbart, begged him to minimize the numbers of deaths in talking to the British because he thought they would not believe it, even though Schwarzbart himself must have been aware of what was going on, as English-language reports on the atrocities were printed in newspapers in London in 1943 and 1944. Nowak also wrote that my mother's cousin Adam Pragier, a member of the Polish government-in-exile in England, told a fellow Jew, Szmul Zygielbojm, to decrease the number of reported Jewish deaths by dropping a zero from a report of 700,000 deaths, as he and others thought that it had to be propaganda. Zygielbojm later died by suicide in protest over the indifference of the Western Allies toward the fate of his fellow Jews.

Together with the difficulty to believe, this pervasive indifference to the fate of the Jews must have played an important part in the lack of intervention. Jan Karski transmitted the pleas of the Jews of Warsaw so that the Allies would take concrete measures to save significant numbers of Jewish people, which would have been possible at least in some territories. The pleas and the information about the atrocities did not bring about any practically meaningful actions, and the reports were actually suppressed, which Nowak writes about as well.

In 1981, Jan Karski reflected on the unique place of the Holocaust in history and of the inaction of the world that silently stood by. In his address at the International Liberators Conference in Washington, D.C., he stated that:

> *The Lord assigned me a role to speak and write*
> *during the war when — as it seemed to me — it*
> *might help. It did not. ...my faith tells me the second*
> *original sin has been committed by humanity:*
> *through commission or omission, or self-imposed*
> *ignorance, or insensitivity, or self-interest, or*
> *hypocrisy, or heartless rationalization. This sin will*
> *haunt humanity to the end of time. It does haunt me.*
> *And I want it to be so.*[2]

Both people and countries that were involved in the Holocaust directly in Europe and the Western Allies in Britain, Canada and the United States continue to find it difficult to confront the incomprehensible horrors of the Holocaust and how they acted during it. To avoid the discomfort of facing it, some diminish it or deny its uniqueness, and some crudely deny that it happened.

Different countries have dealt with the fallout of the Holocaust in their own ways: by facing the past and working to come to terms with it, through reparations and memorialization, or sometimes by denying or avoiding their collaborationist pasts. In many cases, countries struggle between a past divided by both resisters and collaborators. There are also frequent attempts at revising history, and Holocaust denial and distortion is rampant.

Poland has had as much or more difficulties acknowledging what transpired there during and after the war, even going so far as to enact laws enabling censorship of any role at all in war crimes during the Holocaust. Yet, some positive steps are nonetheless being taken.

---

2   E. Thomas Wood and Stanisław M. Jankowski, *Karski: How One Man Tried to Stop the Holocaust* (New York: John Wiley & Sons, Inc., 1994), 255–256.

For example, in 2001, Polish bishops apologized for Polish Catholics' crimes of murder against the Jews. Among several institutions, the Polish Center for Holocaust Research at the Polish Academy of Sciences in Warsaw has chosen another way to discuss the past: their website states that the Holocaust happened on Polish soil in full view of the Polish society and that the Holocaust is an integral part — whether one wants to believe it or not — of Polish history.

For Poles, I think the experience of the Holocaust remains a unique event and carries with it extraordinary responsibilities. Nevertheless, in terms of social awareness, I feel that the Shoah belongs to Jewish rather than to Polish history. Even today, many Poles feel ill at ease, threatened or outright disappointed by Jewish perceptions of the Holocaust, and often the Jews are seen as rivals in the martyrology competition. Too many myths and lies are still finding their way to the public sphere and enter public circulation. In Poland, where there is only a minimal Jewish presence, there are still antisemitic attitudes. However, there is interest in Poland in Jewish culture, as is evident by the engaging and successful museum in Warsaw, POLIN. Various Jewish cultural events are presented by Poles and Jews in annual festivals. A small Jewish community is now active in Poland.

Canada, too, has had to deal with its past — for ignoring the plight of more than nine hundred European Jews aboard the ship MS *St. Louis* in 1939, Canada has been rightly criticized. The refugees' plea for safe haven was refused by Canada, Cuba and other western hemisphere nations. The ship was forced to return to Europe, where more than two hundred Jews later died in camps or from other war-related causes. Former prime minister Jean Chrétien apologized for Canada's abhorrent response to Jewish refugees during the war. In Ottawa in 2000, several Canadian Christian leaders apologized to twenty-five of the MS *St. Louis* survivors. One of the clergymen who apologized to the survivors of the MS *St. Louis* was Doug Blair, a Baptist minister and the great-nephew of Frederick Blair, the bureaucrat who orchestrated Canada's limit on Jewish immigration and who personally advised the government to ignore the pleas of the Jews aboard the *St.*

Louis. In 2011, a monument called the *Wheel of Conscience* was unveiled in Halifax at Pier 21 to commemorate Canada's fateful decision to not let the passengers of *St. Louis* disembark in 1939. And in 2018, prime minister Justin Trudeau formally apologized for Canada's role in turning the ship away from safety.

Canada today is a country that has become a multi-ethnic mosaic and, in my opinion, a sanctuary for the oppressed from various parts of the globe. Canada's previous record on immigration and human rights, however, was very different than it is today. The Canadian government did everything in its power to bar the door to European Jews trying to flee Nazi persecution. Irving Abella and Harold Troper, co-authors of the book *None Is Too Many*, demonstrated using archival research that Canada did less than other Western countries to help the Jews despite mounting reports of Hitler's genocide.

At the heart of the closed-door policy was Frederick Charles Blair, a civil servant, who as the head of immigration in the Mackenzie King administration was in charge of upholding immigration restrictions. His correspondence in federal archives is rife with antisemitic remarks. But Blair did not act in isolation. Mackenzie King, the wartime prime minister, and Vincent Massey, Canada's high commissioner to Britain, supported a tight cap on the number of Jewish immigrants.

Canada's immigration policy did not change appreciably for at least two years after the war ended. The entrenched antisemitic attitudes of the civil servants, politicians and of much of the public continued to resist admission of Jewish people. This approach changed by 1948, as business owners pushed for large immigration to assure adequate supply of labourers and consumers for the expected economic boom. Thus, Canada began admitting refugees and displaced people from several countries, including some Jews, because of the national economic self-interest.

However, a strong, though unspoken, anti-Jewish bias severely limited the numbers of Jews. Jewish groups in Canada continued to be frustrated in their efforts to bring some of the remnants of the

European Jewish people from the displaced persons camps. They finally received an agreement from the government for immigration of tailors and other needleworkers. Even in this case, however, when Canadian officials realized that a large group of primarily Jewish workers would be arriving, they instituted a ruling that no ethnic group could form more than 50 per cent of the workers. It was not until the 1950s that Canada allowed Jews again in large numbers, as had been the case in the 1880s and before World War I.

The attitude of the Canadian government largely reflected Canadian public sentiment toward Jews at the time. Antisemitism was rife throughout Canada and there were concerns that Jewish and other refugees would compete for jobs and not fit into the community. In some places, Jews were not permitted to hold particular jobs, own property or stay in certain hotels, a situation eerily reminiscent of the conditions existing in pre-World War II Poland.

SOURCES

Abella, Irving, and Harold Troper. *None Is Too Many: Canada and the Jews of Europe, 1933–1948*. Toronto: Lester & Orpen Dennys, 1983.

Barsky, Percy. "How 'Numerus Clausus' Was Ended in the Manitoba Medical School." *Canadian Jewish Historical Society Journal*, 1, no. 2. (1977), 75–81.

Engelking, Barbara, and Jacek Leociak, *The Warsaw Ghetto: A Guide to the Perished City*, trans. E. Harris. New Haven: Yale University Press, 2009.

Fater, Issachar. *Yiddishe Muzik in Poiln: Tzvishn Beide Velt-Milkhamos* (Yiddish; Jewish Music in Poland Between the Two World Wars). Tel Aviv: Welt-Federatzie fun Poilishe Yidn, 1970.

Fine, Jonathan. "Anti-Semitism in Manitoba in the 1930s and 40s." *Manitoba History*, no. 32 (1996), 26–33.

Fleming, Michael. *Auschwitz, the Allies and Censorship of the Holocaust*. Cambridge: Cambridge University Press, 2014.

Fuks, Marian. "Musical Traditions of Polish Jews." *Polish Music Journal*. 6, no. 1, Summer 2003. Translated by Maria Piłatowicz.

Fuks, Marian. *Muzyka Ocalona. Judaica polskie*. Warszawa: Wyd. Radia i Telewizji, 1989.

Fuks, Marian, Zygmunt Hoffman, Maurycy Horn, and Jerzy Tomaszewski, eds. *The Polish Jewry: History and Culture*. Warsaw: Interpress Publishers, 1982.

Fukuyama, Francis. *The End of History and the Last Man*. New York: Free Press, 1982.

Fukuyama, Francis. *Our Posthuman Future: Consequences of the Biotechnology Revolution*. New York: Farrar, Straus and Giroux, 2002.

Gilbert, Martin. *Auschwitz and the Allies*. London: Michael Joseph/Rainbird, 1981.

Gutman, Yisrael, and Shmuel Krakowski. *Unequal Victims: Poles and Jews During World War Two*. New York: Holocaust Library, 1986.

Kühl, Stefan. *The Nazi Connection: Eugenics, American Racism and German National Socialism*. New York: Oxford University Press, 1994; quoted in Jeremiah A. Barondess, "Medicine Against Society: Lessons from the Third Reich," JAMA 276, no. 20, (1996): 1657–1661.

Laqueur, Walter. *The Terrible Secret: Suppression of the Truth about Hitler's "Final Solution."* New York: Henry Holt and Company, 1980.

Laqueur, Walter, and Richard Breitman. *Breaking the Silence*. New York: Simon and Schuster, 1986.

Loffman, Morris. "Justice Triumphs: The Eradication of Racial Discrimination at the University of Manitoba Medical College." Address at the 50th reunion of class of 1954, Faculty of Medicine, University of Manitoba, June 2004.

Mendelsohn, Shelomo. *The Battle of the Warsaw Ghetto*. New York: The Yiddish Scientific Institute-YIVO, 1944.

Moore, Terence. "Crumbling Foundation: The Medical School and the Depression." *Manitoba Medicine*, no. 58, (1988): 139–144.

Moore, Terence. "Quotas' End," *Manitoba Medicine*, no. 59 (1989): 29–31.

Nowak, Jan. *Courier from Warsaw*. Detroit: Wayne State University Press, 1982.

Paulsson, Gunnar S. *Secret City: The Hidden Jews of Warsaw, 1940–1945*. New Haven: Yale University Press, 2002.

Rogers, Arnold. Unpublished essay housed in the archives at the Faculty of Medicine, University of Manitoba.

Sandel, Józef. *Umgekumene yidishe kinstler in Poyln* (Yiddish; Jewish Artists in Poland Who Perished). Warsaw: Yidish Bukh, 1957.

Wood, E. Thomas, and Stanisław M. Jankowski. *Karski: How One Man Tried to Stop the Holocaust*. New York: John Wiley & Sons, Inc., 1994.

Index

acculturation, xvi–xvii

Ajzensztadt (Eisenstadt), Marysia ("nightingale of the ghetto"), 27

AK. *See* Armia Krajowa (AK) (Home Army)

Allied forces, 46, 48

Anatomy of the Holocaust and Its Aftermaths (Carter), xxix

Anielewicz, Mordecai (commander of Jewish ghetto fighters), 41, 107

anti-Jewish policies, xix, 22

antisemitism: Canada, 67–68, 120; Manitoba medical school, 68–69; Poland, xviii, 18, 19–20, 33, 56

armband, Star of David, xix, xx, 22, 33

Armia Krajowa (AK) (Home Army), 45

"Aryan": Jews passing as Aryans, 42–43, 123; professional segregation of, xix, xxi; side of Warsaw, xx, xxiii, xxiv, 27, 31, 34, 35, 41–42

Asper Foundation, 118

Asper Jewish Community Campus, 114, 117

assimilation, xvi, xviii

Auschwitz-Birkenau (death camp), 42, 48, 105, 109

Austria: annexation of, 20

Avukah Society (University of Manitoba Medical School), 68–69

Bacterium rosenhauchii, 5

badminton, xxviii, 93

"Ballad" (Centnerszwer), 7

Bauman, Janina (Warsaw ghetto survivor), 110

Beamish, Robert (doctor), 73

Beck, Józef (Polish foreign minister), 21

Belzec (death camp), 48

Ben (family of Juliette Goldenberg), 76

Berney Theatre (Winnipeg), 114

Białystok ghetto, 42, 55, 107, 110, 111

Błyskawica (Polish navy ship), 10

B'nai B'rith, 118, 120

Bonhard, Mrs. (neighbour), 55

Boy-Żeleński, Tadeusz, 35–36

Brenner, Etta, 59, 63, 67

Brokman, Doris (wife of Ryś), 62

Brokman, Janek (Jan) (cousin), 4, 55, 57

Brokman, Karola (née Pragier) (aunt), 4

Brokman, Ryś (Ryszard Magnus) (cousin), 65, 4, 11, 98, 57, 61–62

Brokman, Władek (Władysław) (uncle), 4

Buchenwald (Nazi camp), 58

Building Bridges Conference (Winnipeg), 119–120, 120n2

Burza (Polish navy ship), 10

Canada: antisemitism, 67–69, 120; dispossession of Japanese during World War II, 67; Holocaust Memorial, 102; immigration policy, 60; Jewish community, 101

Canadian Broadcasting Corporation (CBC), 117

Canadian Museum for Human Rights (Winnipeg), xxviii, 118, 120

Carter, Andrew (son), 90, 91, 93, 94, 95, 103–108

Carter, Emilee (née Horn): about, 79–81; Stefan, xxvii–xxviii, 77, 79–80, 94; travel, 90, 99, 108; Winnipeg, life in, 81, 85, 90–91, 113; death, xxviii

Carter, George (cousin), xxxvii, 75, 79. *See also* Rosenhauch, Zdzich (Zdzisław Jerzy) (cousin)

Carter, Joel (son), 85, 91 sports, 92, 93, 94, 99, 94–95, 108–110

Carter, Stefan (pre-war): antisemitism experiences of, 18, 19–20; assimilation, xvi, 19; books, 16–17, 18; education, xvii, xviii, 15–16, 22; family, xvi, 3–7, 9, 11–12, 14; food and drink, 13, 14, 15; friends, 15, 16, 17; hobbies, 8, 16–17, 18; language, 14, 16; Leszno Street (family home), xv, 3, 13; music, 7–8, 16; religion, xvii, 18–19; Smolna Street (family home), 15; travel, xvii, 9–12, 14; Warsaw culture, 8–9, 18

Carter, Stefan (World War II): Lwów, attempted escape to, 23; Warsaw ghetto, xxi–xxiii, 23–27; friends, 22, 26; German factory work, 29; mother sent to Treblinka, 30–31; father remained in Warsaw ghetto, 31; escape from Warsaw ghetto, 31, 33–34; "Aryan" Warsaw, hiding in, 35–36; Warecki, Janek (Jan) (assumed name), 35; letters to Aunt Pola, 36–41; plastic surgery, 42; Warsaw Uprising, 45–46; Pruszków transit camp, 46–47; Łowicz village, 47–48

Carter, Stefan (postwar): reunited with family, 51–52; education, 57, 58, 59, 61, 64–65; last name, changing of, 57; Munich, xxv, 58; immigration to Canada, 62; Winnipeg, xxvii, 63–64, 79; medical school, 67, 69–71, 73; antisemitism, experiences of, 69; awards received, 65, 67, 69, 73,

113; Winnipeg General Hospital, 71–72, 73; Canadian citizenship, 75; New York, 75–77; Mayo Clinic, 77–79, 80–81; research, 73, 77, 82–83, 98; Emilee (wife), xxviii, 77, 79–81, 85, 94, 95; children, 85, 90, 91, 92, 93, 94–95; St. Boniface General Hospital, 79, 81–83; music, 60, 71, 90–92, 114–116; sports, xxviii, 92–94; teaching, 97–98; travel, 98–100; Poland, return visits to, 103–108, 108–110; Holocaust Awareness Committee (HAC), 101–102, 117; Holocaust education, 117–121; death, xxviii

Casey, Tom, 72

"The Cauldron" (September 6, 1942), 30

Centnerszwer, Elżbieta (cousin), 6, 109, 111

Centnerszwer, Maks (Maksymilian) (uncle): Carter's research on, 111; death in Białystok ghetto, 55; music, xvi, xvii–xviii, 6–7, 8, 16, 114

Centnerszwer, Stasia (Stanisława) (aunt) (née Reicher): artist, xvi, 5, 6; death in Białystok ghetto, 55; paintings by, 107, 109, 111–112

Dr. Charlotte W. Ross medal, 73

Chełmno (also Chelmno), 28, 34, 48

Chłodna Street (Warsaw ghetto), xxi, 26, 27

circumcision, 42

"Clarinet Trio" (Mozart), 115

Cohen, Morley (Dr.), 81, 113

Council for Aid to Jews (Żegota), 123

Crimean Sonnets (Mickiewicz), 17

Czajkowska (Szaykowska), Berta, 107, 111, 112

Czechoslovakia: annexation of, 20; Carter's illegal travel to, 58

Czerniaków, Adam (chair of the Judenrat), xxiii, 24, 28

Dachau (Nazi camp), 58

Dar Pomorza (Polish frigate), 10

death camps: Carter's journeys to, 105, 109; children sent to, 29, 100; lack of knowledge of, 2; murder of Jews in gas chambers, 28, 48; outbreaks of resistance, 42. See also specific camps (e.g., Treblinka)

death marches, 48

deportations, xxiii, 28, 29, 30, 105

displaced persons (DP) camps, 57–58, 59, 60

distribution place. See Umschlagplatz

Długa Street (Warsaw), 14

Doupe, Joseph (Dr.), 69–71, 76, 77, 79, 97–98

Duński, Jerzyk (friend), 26

Earth and High Heaven (Graham), 61

Einsatzgruppen (specialized Nazi troops): murder of Jews, Roma, and non-Jewish communists, 28, 48

Elektoralna Street (Warsaw), xxi, 14, 24, 26, 52, 56, 106

Emanuel Ringelblum Jewish

Historical Institute (Warsaw), 105, 106–107, 109

Engelking, Barbara, 112n1

Ethel (family of Juliette Goldenberg), 76, 77

Examining the Holocaust (Canadian Museum for Human Rights exhibit), xxviii

factories. *See* German factories

Falenica (Poland), 21

Feldafing (Germany), 60

"Final Solution," 28–29, 30

Fischer, Ludwig (Warsaw district governor), xx

Fishaut, Ela (friend), 15, 43, 56

Fishaut, Helena (teacher), 15, 43

Fishaut, Piotr (friend), 15

France: declaration of war on Germany, 21

Frank, Hans (Governor General), xxiv

Freeman Family Foundation Holocaust Education Centre, 117–118

Full Catastrophe Living (Kabat-Zinn), 95

Gdańsk (Polish navy ship), 11

Gdynia (Polish navy ship), 11

gentiles: acts of heroism, 5, 34, 108, 121–124, 122n3, 123, 123n4; commemoration of, 100, 117–118

German factories, 25, 29, 30, 31, 48, 107

Germany: annexation of Austria and Czechoslovakia, 20; anti-Jewish policies, xix, 22; "The

Cauldron," 30; factories in Poland, 25, 29, 30, 31, 48, 107; "Final Solution," 28–29, 30; invasion of Poland, 21–22; Soviet Union, attack of, 28; surrender, 48; Warsaw ghetto, 23–24, 25–26

Gerwel, Dr., 99

Gęsia Street prison and concentration camp, 45

"ghetto benches," 20, 68

ghetto fighters (Jewish Combat Organization), 41, 100, 107

Ghetto Fighters' House Museum, 100

ghettoization decree, xxi

ghetto police. *See* Jewish Order Service (police)

Giewont Mountain, 11–12, 105

Goldenberg, Juliette (née Kitzes), 64, 76

Goldenberg, Marcel, 64, 76

Goszer, Barbara, 117

Graszewski, Doctor (Tadzik's alias), 52–54

Great Britain: common defence act with Poland, 20; declaration of war on Germany, 21

Great Synagogue (Warsaw), xvi, xxv, 3, 14

Grom (Polish navy ship), 10

Gross Aktion, xxiii

Gutka (great-aunt), 14, 55

Gypsies. *See* Roma (Gypsies)

Halpern, Stefan (friend), 26, 60, 99

Heart Care Award (St. Boniface Research Centre's Institute of

Cardiovascular Sciences), 113

Hel, Poland, 10

Held, Piotr (friend), 15, 18, 24, 26

Herfurt, Hanna (Hanka) (daughter of Zofia), 34, 45, 53, 57, 99, 110, 118

Herfurt, Zofia, 34, 45, 57

Herfurt-Gerwel, Hanna (Dr.). *See* Herfurt, Hanna (Hanka) (daughter of Zofia)

Hildes, John (Jack) (doctor), 72–73

Hirsch, John (friend), 66

Höfle, Hermann (deportation coordinator, Lublin district), xxiii

Holocaust: education, xxviii–xxix, 101–102, 103, 117–121; lack of knowledge of, 1–2; Holocaust Memorial (Manitoba), 102; survivors, 66, 100, 101; United States Holocaust Memorial Museum (USHMM), 103, 110; Yad Vashem (museum), 99–100, 111, 122

Holocaust Memorial (Manitoba), 102

Home Army. *See* Armia Krajowa (AK) (Home Army)

Horn, Emilee. *See* Carter, Emilee (née Horn)

Human Rights and Holocaust Studies Program (Asper Foundation), 118

identity document, 35

intelligentsia: Jewish, xvii, xix, xxii–xxiii; Polish, 22

Irka (friend), 15, 18

Isbister Scholarship, 65, 67, 69

Israel, 99–100

Jadwiga (Polish navy ship), 11

Jarniewski, Belle (née Millo), 119

Jewish Cemetery (Okopowa Street, Warsaw), 56

Jewish Combat (also Fighting) Organization (ghetto fighters), 107. *See* Warsaw Ghetto Uprising

Jewish Community Centre (Winnipeg), 101

Jewish Council. *See* Judenrat (Jewish Council)

Jewish ghetto fighters (Jewish Combat Organization), 41, 100, 107

Jewish ghetto police. *See* Jewish Order Service (police)

Jewish Heritage Centre (JHC) (Winnipeg), 103, 117–118, 120n2

Jewish Historical Institute (Warsaw). *See* Emanuel Ringelblum Jewish Historical Institute (Warsaw)

Jewish intelligentsia, xvii, xix, xxii–xxiii

Jewish Order Service (police), xxii–xxiii, 24, 28, 30

Jewish school system, xvii–xviii

Jewish Society for the Encouragement of Fine Arts, 6

Jewish Students' Union (UNRRA university), 60

Jewish Symphony Orchestra, 27

Józef, Pan (Mr.) (driver of Pola and Edmund), 7, 55, 86, 104

Judenrat (Jewish Council): exemption from deportations, xxii, 28; policing of Warsaw ghetto, 24; social assistance programs, 25; Warsaw ghetto wall, 23

Kabat-Zinn, Jon, 95

Karmelicka Street (Warsaw), 14

Kaufmann, Walter (conductor), 64

Kennkarte (identity document), 35

Kirschbraun (Kirszbraun), Arnold (professor), 26, 27

Kitzes, Ben, 63, 64, 72, 90, 92

Kitzes, Juliette. See Goldenberg, Juliette (née Kitzes)

Kitzes family (Volodia and Mary), 59–60, 63–64, 81, 90

Kojrański (professor), 26

Kon, Hanka (friend), 15, 56, 110–111

Kon, Mrs. (family friend), 23, 24

Kopel, Staś (Stanisław) (friend), 22, 56, 100

Korczak, Janusz (principal of Warsaw orphanage), 29, 100, 105

Krakow (Poland): Carter's return visits to, 104, 109; postwar, 51–52, 56–57; prison, 34–35

Kraushar, Stefan (friend), 11, 56, 108

Kristallnacht pogrom, 101

Krzeszewska, Danuta (girlfriend of Tadzik), 52, 53, 54, 86, 118

Krzeszewska, Florentyna (mother of Danuta), 54, 86

Łazienki Park (Warsaw), 9, 106, 110

Leist, Ludwig (district governor), xx

Leociak, Jacek, 112n1

Leonka (great-aunt), 14, 55

Leszno Street (Warsaw), xv, 3, 13, 106

letters: Aunt Pola (Pauline) to the Carters, 85–86; from Carter (alias Janek) to Aunt Pola, 36–41; Dr. Milewski-Lipkowski to Aunt Pola, 52–54

Leves, E. (pen name of Adam Rosenblum), 62

Libin (Libera), Zdzisław (professor), 26, 104

Loewi, Otto (Dr.), 76

Loffman, Morris (Dr.), 67

Łowicz (Poland), 47–48

Lubelczyk, Andrew (friend), 29

Lwów (Lviv), 23, 34

Maccabiah Games (Israel), 99

Maclean, John (doctor), 70, 81, 82

MacPherson, Jim (friend), 72

Majdanek (death camp), 48

Manitoba: antisemitism, 67–69, 67n1; Holocaust Memorial, 102; polio epidemic, 72–73; X-ray travelling units, 66

Manitoba Eastern European Heritage Society, 120n2

Manitoba Holocaust Heritage Project, 119

Manitoba Mennonite Historical Society, 120n2

Manitoba Theatre Centre (Royal MTC), 66, 85, 91

Mansbridge, Peter, 2

Maryś (friend of Tadzik and Ryś), 11

Mathers, Alvin T. (dean), 68, 69

Mayo Clinic, 77–79, 80, 81

Mickiewicz, Adam (Polish poet),
    xviii, 17, 98–99, 104
Mila 18 (Uris), 101
Milewski-Lipkowski, Stanisław,
    52–54
Milgrom, Muriel (teacher), 91
Milgrom, Rabbi, 64
Millo, Belle. *See* Jarniewiski, Belle
    (née Millo)
Minsk, Stefan (Wojtek) (friend), 15
Molière, 35–36
Montelupich Street prison
    (Krakow), 34–35
Mościcki, Ignacy (president of
    Poland), 11
Mozart, 27, 114, 115–116
*Mozart: A Meditation on His Life
    and Mysterious Death* (Carter),
    116
Mroszczak, Zofia (friend of Tadzik
    and Zdzich), 35
Munich (Germany), 58–60
Narodowe Siły Zbrojne (National
    Armed Forces), 56
New York: Carter's family in, 59, 61,
    65, 75; Carter's studies in, 75–79,
    80
New York Hospital, 75–76
Nickerson, Mark (Dr.), 73
Nishioka, Hiro (medical student),
    67
"non-Aryan" society, segregation
    of, xix
non-Jewish communists: murder
    of by Einsatzgruppen (Nazi
    troops), 28

Norrie, William, 113
Nowolipie Street (Warsaw ghetto),
    29
Nowy Świat (Polish Morning World),
    86
Nuremberg Code, 78
"Oh My Rosemary," 16, 109
Okopowa Street Jewish Cemetery
    (Warsaw), 56
Operation Reinhard (1941), 28
Order of the Knights of Malta, 52
Orla Street (Warsaw), 14, 106
Otwock (Poland), 22
Pan Tadeusz (Mickiewicz), 17
Pauls, Cheryl, 114
Pawiak Prison (Warsaw), xxiv, 23,
    42, 43, 46
Pawia Street (Warsaw), 23
Pier 21 (Halifax), 62
Piłsudski, Józef, 11, 16, 104
Piłsudski Square (Warsaw), 18, 33
plastic surgery, 42
pogroms, 56, 101
Poland: annexation of parts of
    Czechoslovakia, 20; common
    defence act with Great Britain,
    20; invasion of by Germany, 21;
    navy ships, 10–11, 20; Operation
    Reinhard (1941), 28. *See also*
    Krakow (Poland); Warsaw
    (Poland); Warsaw ghetto;
    Warsaw Uprising (1944)
POLIN (Polish Jewish museum in
    Warsaw), 112
polio epidemic (Manitoba), 72–73
Polish (language), xvi, xvii, 3, 16–17,

104, 123
Polish Center for Holocaust
  Research, 111–112
Poniatowski, Stanisław August
  (Poland's last king), 106
Pragier, Adam (second cousin), xvi,
  19, 48
Pragier, Heniek (Henryk) (uncle), 4
Pragier, Jakub (maternal grandfa-
  ther), 3
Pragier, Janina. See Reicher, Janina
  (mother) (née Pragier)
Pragier, Józio (Józef) (uncle), 4
Pragier, Karola. See Brokman,
  Karola (née Pragier) (aunt)
Pragier, Pola. See Rosenhauch, Pola
  (Pauline) (née Pragier) (aunt)
Pragier, Sara (maternal grand-
  mother), 3
Prowse medal, 73
Pruszków transit camp (Poland),
  46–47, 108–109
Puszet, Alinka (friend), 15, 56
Rabka-Zdrój (Poland), 11, 105
Ramberg, Jaś (friend), 16, 56
Ramberg, Mr. (principal), 16
Rechthand, Genia (Eugenia) (dis-
  tant relative), 14, 25, 56
Rechthand, Kazimierz (distant rela-
  tive, Judenrat member), 14, 24,
  25, 26, 29, 30, 31, 56
Rechthand, Wanda (distant rela-
  tive), 14, 25, 27, 43, 56
Rechthand, Zofia (distant relative),
  14, 25, 29, 30, 56, 86, 99, 100, 106
"Reduta Ordona" (Mickiewicz), 17

Reicher, Dora (paternal grand-
  mother), 5, 25
Reicher, Janina (mother) (née
  Pragier): family, 3–5, 14, 20;
  music, love of, 7, 55; Spójnia
  School, 15; Umschlagplatz, xxviii,
  30–31, 107, 109; Warsaw ghetto,
  24–25, 29
Reicher, Juliusz (paternal grandfa-
  ther), 5, 25
Reicher, Maryla (aunt), 5, 7
Reicher, Stasia (Stanisława).
  See Centnerszwer, Stasia
  (Stanisława) (aunt) (née
  Reicher)
Reicher, Stefan Andrzej (Andrew).
  See Carter, Stefan
Reicher, Wacław (father): chemi-
  cal engineer, 8; family, xvii,
  5–6, 8–9, 106; Judenrat (Jewish
  Council), xxii, 25, 29; music,
  love of, 7; remaining in Warsaw
  ghetto, 31; Warsaw Ghetto
  Uprising, 41
Reicher, Władek (Władysław)
  (uncle), 5, 55
Revisiting the Shadows (Shapiro), 110
Righteous Among the Nations (Yad
  Vashem), 118, 118n1, 122, 123–124
Robinovitch, Sid, 114
Rochwerger, Jan, 105
Roma (Gypsies): murder of by
  Einsatzgruppen (Nazi troops),
  28
Rosenblum, Adam (friend), 61, 62,
  65, 114

Rosenhauch, Edmund (Mundek)
(uncle): family, xvi, 4–5, 11–12;
Cyców, makeshift hospital, 34;
Krakow prison, 34–35; reunion
with Carter, 51–52; Munich, 58;
New York, 59, 61, 65, 75; ophthalmology, 5, 20, 54, 57, 65, 75;
death of, 86; Tadzik, poems and
articles in memory of, 86–89
Rosenhauch, Pola (Pauline) (née
Pragier) (aunt): family, 4–5, 20;
Warsaw, hiding in, 35; letters
from Carter, 36–41; reunion
with Carter, 51–52; Tadzik, death
of, 85–86; Zdzich, search for,
57–58; on mixed marriage, 80;
death of, 86
Rosenhauch, Tadzik (Tadeusz
Edward) (cousin): family, 4,
5, 11, 12; "ghetto bench," 20;
Carter's escape from Warsaw
ghetto, 31, 33–34; "Aryan"
Warsaw, hiding Carter in, 35, 42;
alias (Dr. Graszewski), 52–54;
death of, 52–54, 110; burial, 55;
poem in memory of (by father),
87–89; grave (Stefan's visit to),
104
Rosenhauch, Zdzich (Zdzisław
Jerzy) (cousin): family, 4, 11, 12;
Warsaw, hiding in, 34, 35, 36, 45;
postwar, 54, 57–58, 59, 65. See
also Carter, George (cousin)
Rotholc, Shepsl (boxing champion),
8, 24
Royal MTC, 66

Różycka, Zofia, 35–36, 42, 47, 118
Santayana, George, 105
Saski (Saxon) Garden (Warsaw), 18,
33, 52, 106
Schneid, Otto (artist, art historian),
6
schools, secret in Warsaw ghetto,
26, 27, 29, 60, 90
Second Generation Group of
Winnipeg, 103
secret schools (Warsaw ghetto). See
schools, secret in Warsaw ghetto
secularization, xvii
Sendler, Irena, 123
Shapiro, Irene (Warsaw and
Białystok ghetto survivor), 110
Sheps, Sheldon (friend), 79
Smocza Street (Warsaw ghetto),
29, 30
smuggling: assets, xxii; food in
Warsaw ghetto, 24
Sobibor (death camp), 42, 48
Society for Supporting Agriculture
(Toporol). See Toporol (Society
for Supporting Agriculture)
Soviet Union: areas occupied by,
23, 34, 55; army advancing, 45,
48, 51; attack of by Germany,
28; death marches, 48; Warsaw
Uprising, lack of help in, 46
Spielberg, Steven, 103
Śpiew (Singing) (Centnerszwer), 6
Spójnia (Union) School, 14, 15–16,
26, 56, 100, 106
Star of David armband, xix, xx, 22,
33

starvation: effects of, research on in
Warsaw ghetto, 26
St. Boniface General Hospital
(Winnipeg), 79, 81–83, 98, 113
Stone, Daniel, 110
"Symphony" (Rosenblum as E.
Leves), 62, 114
Szaykowska, Berta. *See* Czajkowska
(Szaykowska), Berta
"tale of two cities," xv–xvi, xx, xxiv–
xxv, 1
Tatra Mountains, xvii, 11, 20, 105
The Holocaust Remembered (bian-
nual newsletter), 117
*The Warsaw Ghetto: A Guide to the
Perished City* (Engelking and
Leociak), 112n1
Thomas Fisher Rare Book Library
(University of Toronto), 6
"Three Budrys" (Mickiewicz), 17
Tłomackie Street (Warsaw), xvi, 3,
14
Tom, Ewa (teacher), 26, 27
Tomb of the Unknown Soldier
(Warsaw), 18, 106
Toporol (Society for Supporting
Agriculture), xxii, 26–27
Treblinka (death camp): children
sent to, 29, 100; killing of Jews
by gas chamber, 28, 48; outbreak
of resistance, 42; Stefan's visits
to, 105, 109; "The Cauldron," 30
Trenkler, Waldemar (boarder), 15,
22
"Tristan" (Centnerszwer), 7
Tworki hospital (Poland), 47, 51

U Fukiera (winery), xvii, 8, 106
Umschlagplatz (distribution place),
xxviii, 28, 30–31, 107, 109
United Nations Relief and
Rehabilitation Administration
(UNRRA) University, 59, 60,
61
United States Holocaust Memorial
Museum (USHMM), 103, 110
University of Manitoba: antisemi-
tism, 67–69; Carter's studies,
64–65
UNRRA. *See* United Nations
Relief and Rehabilitation
Administration (UNRRA)
University
Unto Every Person There Is a Name
(B'nai B'rith), 118
Uris, Leon, 101
USHMM. *See* United States
Holocaust Memorial Museum
(USHMM)
Vogel, Gerry (Dr.), 79
*Voices of Winnipeg Holocaust
Survivors*, 119
Wanda (Polish navy ship), 11
Warecki, Janek (Jan) (Carter's as-
sumed name), 35
Warsaw (Poland): "Aryan" side
of, xx, xxiii, xxiv, 27, 31, 34, 35,
41–42; assimilated Jews, xvi–
xviii; German occupation, xix,
21–24; interwar, xviii; postwar,
51; pre-war, xv, 9; school system,
xvii. *See also* Warsaw ghetto;
Warsaw Uprising (1944)

Warsaw ghetto: borders, movement of by German authorities, 25–26; conditions, 24, 25; creation of, xx–xxi, 23; deportation order, 28, 29, 30; *Gross Aktion* (deportation to Treblinka), xxiii; Jewish Combat Organization (ghetto fighters), 41, 100, 107; Jewish Order Service (police), xxii–xxiii, 24, 28, 30; Judenrat (Jewish Council), xxii, 23; secret schools, 26, 27, 29, 60, 90; starvation, research on the effects of, 26; *Umschlagplatz* (distribution place), xxviii, 28, 30–31, 107, 109; underground culture, 27; underground Jewish archives, 106–107. *See also* Warsaw Ghetto Uprising (April 1943)

Warsaw Ghetto Database, 112

Warsaw Ghetto Uprising (April 1943), xxv, 41–42, 52–54, 101, 107, 117

Warsaw Rising Museum, 54, 112

Warsaw Uprising (1944), xxv, 45–46

Weiss, Philip (HAC chairman), 101–102, 117

Werier, Val (journalist), 90

Werier family, 64

Wicher (Polish navy ship), 10, 20

Wieliczka ghetto, 34

Wiesel, Elie, 2

Winkler, Gerry (friend), 75, 77

Winnipeg: antisemitism, 67–68, 69; arts and culture, 85, 90–92, 113–116; Carter's arrival in, 63–64; Carter's sponsorship to, 59–60; Holocaust education, 117–121; Jewish community, 101–102, 103, 110; Jewish Heritage Centre, 103

Winnipeg Blue Bombers, 63, 72

Winnipeg General Hospital, 71–72, 73

Winnipeg Masters Badminton Championships, xxviii

Winnipeg Symphony Orchestra, 64

Winnipeg Tribune, 90

Winter in the Morning (Bauman), 110

Witold, Mr. (friend of Miss Różycka), 36, 47

Wojtyła, Karol (future Pope John Paul II), 12

Wood (Dr.), 77–78

Wright, Irving (doctor), 75

X-ray travelling units (Manitoba), 66

Yad Vashem (World Holocaust Remembrance Center), 100, 111, 122

Yiddish, xvi, 5, 14, 19

Yom HaShoah, 101, 102, 118

Young Men's Hebrew Association (YMHA). *See* Jewish Community Centre (Winnipeg)

Zakopane (Poland), 11–12, 20, 105

Żegota (underground organization), 123

Zentner, Hersch, 117

Fondation Azrieli Foundation

The Azrieli Foundation was established in 1989 to realize and extend the philanthropic vision of David J. Azrieli, C.M., C.Q., M.Arch. The Foundation's mission is to support a wide spectrum of initiatives in education and research. The Azrieli Foundation is an active supporter of programs in the fields of education, the education of architects, scientific and medical research, and the arts. The Azrieli Foundation's many initiatives include: the Holocaust Survivor Memoirs Program, which collects, preserves, publishes and distributes the written memoirs of survivors in Canada; the Azrieli Institute for Educational Empowerment, an innovative program successfully working to keep at-risk youth in school; the Azrieli Fellows Program, which promotes academic excellence and leadership on the graduate level at Israeli universities; the Azrieli Music Project, which celebrates and fosters the creation of high-quality new Jewish orchestral music; and the Azrieli Neurodevelopmental Research Program, which supports advanced research on neurodevelopmental disorders, particularly Fragile X and Autism Spectrum Disorders.